Oxford School Shakespeare

The Taming of the Shrew

Edited by

Roma Gill
M.A. *Cantab.*, B. Litt. *Oxon*

Oxford University Press

Oxford University Press, Walton Street, Oxford OX2 6DP

Oxford   New York   Toronto
Delhi   Bombay   Calcutta   Madras   Karachi
Petaling Jaya   Singapore   Hong Kong   Tokyo
Nairobi   Dar es Salaam   Cape Town
Melbourne   Auckland

and associated companies in
Berlin   Ibadan

Oxford is a trade mark of Oxford University Press

© Oxford University Press 1990
This revised edition first published 1992
Reprinted 1993

ISBN 0 19 831976 2

Illustrations by Alexy Pendle.

Cover photograph by Laurence Burns shows Vanessa Redgrave as
Katherina, and Timothy Dalton as Petruchio, in Theatr Clwyd's 1986
production of *The Taming of the Shrew*.

For Laura

Oxford School Shakespeare
edited by Roma Gill

A Midsummer Night's Dream
Romeo and Juliet
As You Like It
Macbeth
Julius Caesar
The Merchant of Venice
Henry IV Part 1
Twelfth Night
The Taming of the Shrew
Othello
Hamlet

Printed in Great Britain at the University Press, Cambridge

Contents

Contents

Introduction

On stage and on screen *The Taming of the Shrew* is an outstanding comic success. In performance, the characters are instantly recognizable; and all the disguisings and mistakings, which seem so laborious when they are explained to a reader, are immediately apparent to an *audience*. When the play is acted, it moves with great speed through the complications of its plot. Spectators are probably not conscious of the extreme complexity of the plotting and characterization—a complexity which is even more remarkable when we remember that this is one of Shakespeare's earliest plays, and perhaps his first attempt at writing comedy!

The Taming of the Shrew could be described as 'an-action-within-a-plot-within-a-deception'. The 'deception' involves a tinker —Christopher Sly—and an English nobleman. The 'plot' concerns an Italian gentleman—Lucentio—and his efforts to win the fair Bianca to be his wife. And the 'action' is Petruchio's 'taming' of the 'shrew', Katherina.

1. *The deception*

Shakespeare is on home ground at the opening of his play, setting the scene in Warwickshire, not far from where he was born in Stratford-upon-Avon. The geography is clear from the tinker Sly's reference to his origin at 'Burton-heath' and his acquaintance with 'Marian Hacket the fat ale-wife of Wincot'—who was quite possibly a real person. Both Sly and the unnamed Lord returning from the day's hunting are, we can assume, fairly typical of their contemporaries in Elizabethan society. The distinction of social classes is marked as soon as the Lord speaks, and the Huntsmen reply to him, in the blank verse used dramatically to indicate superior characters or elevated topics[1]. The contrast between the 'prosaic' Sly and the 'poetic' Lord is further emphasized when the Huntsmen are given directions for Sly's accommodation in 'the fairest chamber', and the play-acting theme is heightened by the arrival of the actors' touring company.

Such strolling players were regular visitors to English country houses (and country inns) during the summer months. The London

---

[1] See 'Shakespeare's Verse', p. xvi.

theatres were usually closed to avoid the spreading of infectious diseases, and the actors must tour, or else disband their companies. The Lord is familiar with the company—and also it seems, with some contemporary acting techniques. He directs his page to play the Lady's part, just as any boy-actor would perform female roles in the Elizabethan theatre (where apprentice boys always acted the women's parts), and we also learn the correct behaviour for a lady, who should present herself 'With soft low tongue and lowly courtesy'.

Two cultures collide when Sly wakes and tries to establish his own identity and social sphere against the opposition of the Servingmen who try to convince him of his noble origins. The Servingmen are successful—partly, perhaps, because Sly has always aspired to the nobility: after all, he told the Hostess who threw him out of her ale-house that his family 'came in with Richard Conqueror'. When Sly has accepted his new role (even attempting to speak in the appropriate manner), Shakespeare manipulates the characters—just for a laugh—into a tricky situation in which the tinker insists that his new-found 'lady' should come to bed. The arrival of the players rescues the terrified Bartholomew, and sustains the Lord's deception with their own illusion—*their* play. Sly—who has taken the leading part until now—retires to become, together with the Lord and the Servingmen, an audience for a completely new play. He is allowed some critical comment on the scene that follows—''Tis a very excellent piece of work, madam lady. Would 'twere done!'—and then Sly, with the Lord's deception, is forgotten[2].

2.   *The plot*

All that we have already learned about the Warwickshire Lord and the manner of his living—the courtly behaviour of his servants and the refined elegance of his furnishings and pictures—should lead us to expect that he will have an equally sophisticated taste in drama. Fortunately, the players are able to provide suitable entertainment. Their play, which tells the story of Lucentio, is loosely based on a classical Italian comedy, *I Suppositi* (The Impostors) by Ariosto, which was translated into English by George Gascoigne in 1566 and given the title *Supposes*. The *dramatis personae* of *Supposes* are the stock characters of the Latin comedy, and so is the theme—the attempt of a young man (aided by his clever servant) to secure the girl he loves, although her father favours a rival who is richer—and much older.

---

[2]   See appendix A, p. 101.

The first exchanges between Lucentio and Tranio make sure that we know that the scene is now Italy—Padua—and that these are 'really' actors. They speak formal blank verse, in contrast to the relaxed idiom of Sly's speeches, and speak for the audience to hear, not to converse with each other. The atmosphere relaxes, becoming more 'natural', when Baptista, his daughters, and Bianca's suitors erupt on to the scene, producing a little drama for which Lucentio and Tranio become the audience, until finally Lucentio decides to join the rival suitors and be a competitor for Bianca's love—whilst Tranio, disguised as his master, plays the part of Lucentio. In later scenes Tranio tries to speak as though he were indeed the master and not a servant: his use of learned similes and contorted syntax should be taken as the equivalent of an upper-class accent:

> Fair Leda's daughter had a thousand wooers;
> Then well one more may fair Bianca have,
> And so she shall: Lucentio shall make one,
> Though Paris came in hope to speed alone.

> (*1*, 2, 241–4)

Tranio is 'talking posh'.

The confrontation of the rival suitors comes in *Act 2*, Scene 1, when Gremio and the supposed Lucentio (who is Tranio in disguise), compete for Bianca's hand in response to her father's promise that 'he of both That can assure my daughter greatest dower Shall have my Bianca's love'. It seems that Bianca is being sold to the highest bidder—but this is not, in fact, the case.

It was the duty of an Elizabethan father to look after his daughter, making certain that she married a husband who would be able to support her in comfort and who would be generous in providing for his wife's future should he himself die. The Elizabethan lady had few legal rights: when she married, she and everything she owned (the money she inherited from her father, for instance) became the property of her husband—and there were no careers open to women.

Baptista is acting responsibly—although, of course, he is being duped by Tranio. His conduct here, in arranging the marriage of Bianca (their father's 'treasure', according to Katherina in 2, 1, 32) justifies his earlier treatment of his elder daughter, when he accepted Petruchio's offer of marriage in what seems to be the main business of *The Taming of the Shrew*.

3.   *The action—the taming of the shrew*
Stories of nagging and unruly wives—shrews (the modern equivalent, I suppose, is 'bitch')—are common in early ballad

literature and folk-tales, although Shakespeare seems to have no such particular source for the story of Katherina and Petruchio. In popular fiction, the husband's triumph is secured (to male applause) through the use of brute force—but Shakespeare is sparing with physical violence. Early in their encounter Katherina tempts her suitor when he claims to be a gentleman. She strikes him—but Petruchio contents himself with the warning: 'I swear I'll cuff you if you strike again'. And his warning is heeded (2, 1, 222).

Petruchio's method of 'taming' Katherina seems cruel: he drags her away from her own wedding-feast, and insists upon an uncomfortable journey to his own house; she is cold and tired—but food and sleep are denied. And all the time Petruchio assures his wife that he is acting in her best interests: he declares the wedding guests too rough, the dinner inedible, and the new clothes unbecoming. It is, he tells us, the way 'to kill a wife with kindness'. At the end of *Act 4*, Scene 1 Petruchio lets the audience into his secret, speaking of Katherina as his 'falcon' and of the technique he will use to 'man [his] haggard'. The terms would have been familiar to Shakespeare's audience, who were acquainted with the sport of hawking which needed a wild bird, made gentle, and subdued to the will of the trainer, but still keen to hunt and catch for him—see Appendix B, p. 104. Anyone who has read the novel *A Kestrel for a Knave*, written by Barry Hines in 1968 (and subsequently made into the film, 'Kes'), will recognize what is happening—and will understand, too, that the process cannot be effected without some strain on the part of the self-appointed falconer, who must share the hawk's discipline.

In the management of Katherina there are three stages, and each one is signalled by a kiss. The first kiss is that of a triumphant hunter who has secured his bird. On his very first appearance Petruchio openly stated his intention 'to wive it wealthily in Padua', and not all his friend's warnings can shake his resolution. He is not even deterred by the exhibition of Katherina's temper when she breaks the lute over Hortensio's head. When Katherina comes to meet him on the stage, Petruchio advances warily, as though stalking his prey; then he gently caresses her with words of love. Katherina struggles, at first verbally and then with attempted physical strength—which Petruchio easily resists. Another round of insults is followed by more loving words, and after a brief final round Petruchio assumes the victor's part: 'I must and will have Katherina for my wife'. Petruchio sustains the new role he has created for himself until the formalities with Baptista are concluded, and he can celebrate the first part of his conquest: 'kiss me, Kate, we will be married o' Sunday'.

This kiss is almost a violation. Katherina does not speak; she leaves the stage at the same time as Petruchio, but probably at a different stage door.

The second kiss is a different matter. It is first asked, then refused, and then allowed. Katherina has endured the shame of her marriage to a disorderly ruffian, and suffered the deprivations of her new home life. She has even allowed Petruchio to determine sun and moon—the day and the night—for her:

> . . . sun it is not, when you say it is not,
> And the moon changes even as your mind

— although the second line here permits her to impute a degree of lunacy to her husband's conduct. Her obedience has been tested in the embarrassing encounter with the fellow-traveller (who proves to be Vincentio, the father of Lucentio), and she has shown a new charm—even a sense of fun—in sharing in her husband's deception. For Petruchio, this was a kind of 'trial run', to test the success of his training.

The relationship between Katherina and Petruchio has changed. We know this when the party arrives outside Lucentio's house, where the real Vincentio confronts the supposed Vincentio. As soon as the comedy begins, Petruchio draws his wife to the side: 'Prithee, Kate, let's stand aside and see the end of this controversy'. In becoming an audience, apart from the action they are now watching, Katherina and Petruchio are brought together: their separation from the other characters emphasizes their mutual togetherness.

And the second kiss, which comes at the end of *Act 5*, Scene 1, when there is only a servant to witness it, is the kiss of confederates. Petruchio and Katherina are ready for their big scene.

The joyous celebration of a triple wedding needs no explanation. A note of discord is struck by Hortensio's widow, a character who seems to have been something of an afterthought on Shakespeare's part. The spirited exchange between her and Katherina shows Petruchio's 'taming' has not broken his wife's spirit—but now both husband and wife enjoy the wrangling that ensues. It is a game, one that all the husbands relish—especially when it develops into the testing situation where the men can lay their bets, each backing his own wife against the other two women. What starts as homely festival fun becomes serious when Katherina wins Petruchio's bet for him. For the theatre audience, the outcome of the wager was never in doubt; the defeated husbands take their losses in good part, and the wives enjoy their discomfiture—when Lucentio rues his loss, Bianca has no sympathy: 'The more fool you for laying on my duty'. But then Petruchio takes charge, and puts Katherina in the position of command to deliver his lecture, the fruits of her learned experience.

The speech is made up of Elizabethan commonplaces about the duty of a wife—utterances which have their basis in the marriage service of the Church of England and in the homily 'Of the State of Matrimony' which was preached annually[1]; ultimately, of course, these derive from the authority of the New Testament. Modern audience reactions to this speech are many and varied—as indeed are the emphases of actresses and theatrical directors. The lines have been delivered with heavy irony, implying that Petruchio's triumph is illusory; or with spiritless submission, suggesting that the victory has been dearly bought, and that 'a Kate Conformable as other household Kates' (2, 1, 276–7) is really not much fun.

I myself prefer to take the speech at its face value, recognizing its historical context and its general truths, and anticipating the third kiss, which announces the consummation of a relationship: 'Come on and kiss me Kate . . .

    Come, Kate, we'll to bed.
    We three are married, but you two are sped.'

The play limps disappointingly in its final couplet, tempting a critic to refer to Shakespeare's inexperience as a dramatist at the time he wrote *The Taming of the Shrew* (>1592), and suggesting that he was not in perfect control of the very complicated material that he had chosen to work with. We have come a long way from the Warwickshire (England) alehouse of the Induction's first scene; Christopher Sly, the trickster Lord, and the touring actors have all been forgotten in the interest generated by the play's 'real' characters—a man, and a boy dressed as a woman, whose action and moral dilemmas are more important today than they were to their first audience.

<hr/>

[1] See 'Background', p. 119.

Leading characters in the play

1 *THE DECEPTION*

Christopher Sly   *a drunken peasant in Warwickshire (England) who is persuaded that he is a nobleman.*

Lord   *a real nobleman, who plays a trick on* Sly.

2 *THE PLOT*

Lucentio   *a young gentleman visiting Padua, who falls in love with* Bianca.

Baptista   *a wealthy citizen of Padua who wants to find suitable husbands for his two daughters.*

Katherina   Baptista's *elder daughter, who seems unlikely to get a husband because of her bad temper (but see* 'The Action', *below).*

Bianca   Baptista's *younger daughter;* Hortensio *and* Gremio *both want to marry her, and* Lucentio *falls in love with her.*

Petruchio   Hortensio's *friend, visiting Padua in search of a rich wife (see* 'The Action', *below).*

3 *THE ACTION*

Katherina   Baptista's *elder daughter, whose intelligence and independence make her resent the way she is treated by her father and her sister's suitors. She challenges* Petruchio, *but is finally persuaded to accept his superior strength.*

Petruchio   *a stranger from Verona, who has come to Padua hoping to find a rich wife. He engages in a battle with* Katherina, *refusing to let her rest until she gives in to him.*

The Taming of the Shrew: the play

Induction

Scene 1   Christopher Sly, in a drunken sleep outside an English country pub, is discovered by a noble Lord returning from a day's hunting. The Lord decides to play a trick on Sly. He takes him home, and instructs the servants to treat Sly as though he were a nobleman who has been sick and out of his mind. A company of travelling players arrives at the Lord's house.

Scene 2   Sly wakes up, and is persuaded to watch the actors perform their play—which is:

The Taming of the Shrew.

Act 1

Scene 1   Lucentio arrives in Padua with his manservant, Tranio. They encounter Baptista with his two daughters, Katherina and Bianca. Baptista insists that a husband must be found for Katherina (the elder daughter) before he will allow anyone to marry Bianca. Bianca's suitors, Hortensio and Gremio, call a truce in their rivalry for Bianca's love—but now Lucentio has fallen in love with her, too. He decides to change places with Tranio, so that he can attend on Bianca disguised as a schoolmaster—whilst Tranio (calling himself 'Lucentio') will also present himself as a suitor to Bianca.

Scene 2   Petruchio arrives in Padua with his servant, Grumio. They call on Hortensio, and Petruchio explains that he is hoping to find a rich wife. When he hears about Katherina, Petruchio declares that she will be the right wife for him!
Whilst they are talking, Gremio comes along with Lucentio, who is now disguised as a schoolmaster (calling himself 'Cambio'). Gremio and Hortensio renew their rivalry for Bianca's love—and they are joined by a third competitor, who calls himself 'Lucentio' (but who, in fact, is Tranio in disguise).

Act 2

Scene 1   Katherina and Bianca are quarrelling. Tranio ('Lucentio') and Petruchio introduce themselves to Baptista, and Petruchio begins his wooing of Katherina. They fight, but he is determined to marry her. Gremio and Tranio ('Lucentio') make bids for the hand of Bianca; Gremio is defeated—but 'Lucentio' must get his father to secure the promises he has made.

Act 3

Scene 1   Bianca's suitors present themselves to her as tutors: Lucentio is disguised as 'Cambio', and Hortensio is the musician, 'Litio'.

Scene 2   On the wedding day, Baptista waits with his daughters (and Bianca's suitors) for the arrival of Katherina's bridegroom. Biondello describes Petruchio's appearance, and the bridal party goes off to the church. Lucentio and Tranio stay behind. Gremio returns to report what has happened in the church. Petruchio and Katherina—now married—come back with their friends; but Petruchio refuses to wait for the marriage-feast, and he insists on carrying away his bride.

Act 4

Scene 1   Petruchio's servants are preparing to receive their master and his new wife. Grumio describes their journey from Padua. Petruchio complains about their dinner, and Katherina goes hungry to bed. Petruchio outlines the method he will use for 'taming' his 'shrew'.

Scene 2   Hortensio ('Litio') and Tranio ('Lucentio') listen whilst the *real* Lucentio ('Cambio') courts Bianca. They both agree to withdraw from the competition for Bianca's love, and Hortensio announces that he is going to marry a rich widow. Tranio tells Lucentio that he has won Bianca—provided that he can get his father's support (which Baptista demanded in *Act 2*, Scene 1). A passing Pedant is persuaded to impersonate Vincentio, Lucentio's father.

Scene 3   Petruchio continues the 'taming' of Katherina, refusing to let her eat, and sending away her new clothes. He plans to return to Baptista's house—but will not go until Katherina agrees with him in everything he says.

Scene 4   Tranio ('Lucentio') introduces the Pedant—who is pretending to be his father ('Vincentio')—to Baptista. They go to draw up the marriage-settlement for Bianca. Biondello tells the *real* Lucentio ('Cambio') that he must now take Bianca to the church and find a priest to marry them.

Scene 5   Katherina tries once more to contradict her husband, then finally concedes victory to Petruchio. They depart for Padua, and on the way they meet the *real* Vincentio, the father of Lucentio.

Act 5

Scene 1   Lucentio and Bianca hurry off to the church. Petruchio, Katherina, and the *real* Vincentio arrive at Lucentio's house, but the Pedant (who is *pretending* to be Lucentio's father) refuses to let them in. Lucentio and Bianca, newly married, return; and the false identities are revealed.

Scene 2   A marriage-feast has been enjoyed, honouring three wedded couples: Petruchio and Katherina; Lucentio and Bianca; Hortensio and his wealthy Widow. The three brides leave the room, and the husbands lay bets on which of their wives will prove the most obedient. Katherina wins the wager for Petruchio, and delivers a lecture on the proper duty of a wife to her husband.

Shakespeare's Sources

Shakespeare took his raw material for *The Taming of the Shrew* from a variety of sources. The deception of Christopher Sly derives ultimately from *The Arabian Nights*. Shakespeare could have read a version of this in a collection of stories by Richard Edwards, which was published in 1570 but which is now lost. Lucentio's plot to win Bianca comes from George Gascoigne's *Supposes* (1566), which is itself a translation of *I Suppositi* by Ariosto. No single source has been found for the main action, although it is possible that Shakespeare knew the ballad of *A Shrewde and Curste Wyfe* which was published in 1550. Here, as in Shakespeare's play, the 'shrew' is compared to a docile sister, her wedding is disrupted, and she is similarly deprived of food.

Date and Text

It is impossible to assign a precise date to *The Taming of the Shrew*. Shakespeare's play is clearly related to an anonymous play, *The Taming of A Shrew*, and it seems most likely that the unknown author was the borrower, and that *A Shrew* is later than *The Shrew*. *A Shrew* was published in 1594 and may have been written as early as 1592. *The Taming of the Shrew* was not published until 1623, when it appeared in the collection of Shakespeare's plays which is known as the First Folio.

Shakespeare's Verse

Shakespeare's plays are mainly written in 'blank verse', the form preferred by most dramatists in the sixteenth and early seventeenth centuries. It is a very flexible medium, which is capable—like the human speaking voice—of a wide range of tones. Basically the lines, which are unrhymed, are ten syllables long. The syllables have alternating stresses, just like normal English speech; and they divide into five 'feet'. The technical name for this is 'iambic pentameter'.

Lord
What's hére? One deád, or drúnk? See, dóth he bréathe?

Second Huntsman
He breáthes, my lórd. Were hé not warmed with
  ále,
This were a béd but cóld to sleép so soúndly.

Lord
O monstrous beást, how like a swine he liés!
Grim deáth, how foúl and loáthsome is thine image!
Sirs, Í will práctise on this drúnken mán.
What think you, íf he were conveyed to béd.
Wrapped in sweet clóthes, rings pút upon his
  fingers,
A móst delícious banquet bý his béd,
And bráve attendants neár him when he wakés.
Would nót the béggar thén forgét himsélf?

First Huntsman
Beliéve me, lórd, I think he cánnot choóse.

(*1*, 1, 28–39)

The pentameter accommodates a variety of speech tones—the Lord's surprise when he discovers Sly in his drunken sleep, his disgust when he realizes what he has found, and his delight in the practical joke that he plans. The Huntsman replies politely to his master; and the regularity of his lines shows him to belong to the Lord's society. Although he is a servant, he is not—like Sly and the Hostess—a peasant.

In this quotation, the lines are mainly regular in length and normal in iambic stress pattern. Sometimes Shakespeare deviates from the norm, writing lines that are longer or shorter than ten syllables, and varying the stress patterns for unusual emphasis—as in the Lord's cry of exaggerated horror, 'Grim deáth, how foúl and loáthsome iś thine iḿage!'. The verse line sometimes contains the grammatical unit of meaning—'O moństrous beaśt, how liḱe a swíne he liés!'—thus allowing for a pause at the end of the line, before a new idea is started; at other times, the sense runs on from one line to the next, as it does in lines 122–3, where the Lord speaks of 'a wóman's gíft To raín a shower óf commańded teárs'. This makes for the natural fluidity of speech, avoiding monotony but still maintaining the iambic rhythm.

Characters in the Play

The Induction
in
WARWICKSHIRE

Christopher Sly	*a tinker*
Hostess	*at the alehouse*
Lord	
Bartholomew, the Lord's page	
Huntsmen	
and	*attending the* Lord
Servingmen	
Actors	*visiting the* Lord, *and playing the parts of the characters in*

THE TAMING OF THE SHREW

THE FATHERS
Baptista Minola	*a rich citizen of Padua*
Vincentio	*a merchant from Pisa*

THE DAUGHTERS
Katherina	*the 'shrew',* Baptista's *elder daughter*
Bianca	Baptista's *younger daughter*

THE SUITORS
Gremio	*a rich old man of Padua*
Hortensio	*a gentleman of Padua*
Lucentio	*a gentleman from Pisa*
Petruchio	*a gentleman from Verona*

THE SERVANTS
Tranio	*servant to* Lucentio
Biondello	Lucentio's *boy*
Grumio	*servant to* Petruchio
Curtis	*servant at* Petruchio's *house*

ALSO
Tailor
Haberdasher
Pedant from Mantua
Widow
Additional Servants

The scene of the play is Italy

Induction

Induction

This technique for opening a play was often used in the 16th and early 17th centuries — although Shakespeare never again attempts it, and even seems to lose interest here after he has started off the main action of *The Shrew*.

Scene 1

Christopher Sly quarrels with the Hostess who is throwing him out of the tavern. He falls into a drunken sleep, and is discovered by a nobleman who is on his way home from hunting, discussing the day's sport and the performance of his hounds. The Lord decides to play a trick on Sly when he wakes; and so the drunkard is carried to the Lord's house. When a company of actors arrives, the Lord involves them in his plan.

Scene 1

Enter Christopher Sly *and the* Hostess

Sly
I'll feeze you, in faith.

Hostess
A pair of stocks, you rogue!

Sly
You're a baggage, the Slys are no rogues. Look in the Chronicles, we came in with Richard Conqueror. Therefore *paucus pallibris*, let the world slide. Sessa!

Hostess
You will not pay for the glasses you have burst?

Sly
No, not a denier. Go by, Saint Jeronimy, go to thy cold bed and warm thee.

1 *feeze*: fight, frighten.
2 *pair of stocks*: The Hostess threatens to
   punish Sly by locking him in the stocks,
   where he would be confined by the ankles
   and exposed to public ridicule.
4 *Chronicles*: history books.
   we . . . Conqueror: Sly boasts of his
   family's history — but he has got the
   phrase wrong, mistaking the Christian
   name and assuming that 'Conqueror' is a
   family name.
5 *paucus pallabris*: less of your talking; Sly
   uses a phrase made famous in a play, *The
   Spanish Tragedy*, by one of Shakespeare's
   contemporaries, Thomas Kyd.
   let . . . slide: why worry.
   Sessa: give over
6 *burst*: broken.
7 *not a denier*: not a penny (a 'denier' was
   the smallest French coin).
   Go by, Saint Jeronimy: Sly again recalls a
   popular catchphrase from *The Spanish
   Tragedy*, whose hero (in Sly's mind
   confused with Saint Jerome) warns
   himself 'Hieronimo beware; go by, go by'.
9 *thirdborough*: constable; the Hostess uses a
   Warwickshire term.
11 *boy*: A term of general contempt.
12 *and kindly*: and welcome.
12s.d. *winding*: blowing.
   from hunting: The Lord has probably been
   hunting hares (compare the mention of
   'the hedge corner' at line 17); the men —
   huntsmen and servingmen — would be on
   foot, with the hounds leashed in couples.

13 *charge*: order.
   tender well: take good care of.
14 *Breathe Merriman*: let Merriman (the
   name of a hound) have a rest.
   embossed: foaming at the mouth, quite
   exhausted.
15 *couple*: leash.
   deep-mouthed brach: bitch with a deep
   voice (presumably, also, experienced;
   young hounds were leashed with older
   ones for training purposes).
16 *made it good*: picked up the scent.
17 *in the coldest fault*: at the worst break.
20 *cried upon it*: gave tongue (i.e. to show
   that he had found the scent).
   the merest loss: when it was completely
   lost.

Hostess
I know my remedy, I must go fetch the thirdborough.   [*Exit*
   Sly
10 Third, or fourth, or fifth borough, I'll answer him
   by law. I'll not budge an inch, boy. Let him come,
   and kindly.

   He falls asleep. There is a winding of horns.
   Enter a Lord *from hunting, with his train.*

   Lord
Huntsman, I charge thee tender well my hounds.
Breathe Merriman — the poor cur is embossed —
15 And couple Clowder with the deep-mouthed brach.
Saw'st thou not, boy, how Silver made it good
At the hedge corner, in the coldest fault?
I would not lose the dog for twenty pound.
   First Huntsman
Why, Bellman is as good as he, my lord:
20 He cried upon it at the merest loss,
And twice today picked out the dullest scent;
Trust me, I take him for the better dog.
   Lord
Thou art a fool: if Echo were as fleet,
I would esteem him worth a dozen such.

21 *dullest*: faintest.
23 *fleet*: fast.

25 But sup them well, and look unto them all;
    Tomorrow I intend to hunt again.
        First Huntsman
    I will, my lord.
        Lord
    What's here? One dead, or drunk? See, doth he
    breathe?
        Second Huntsman
    He breathes, my lord. Were he not warmed with ale,
30 This were a bed but cold to sleep so soundly.
        Lord
    O monstrous beast, how like a swine he lies!
    Grim death, how foul and loathsome is thine image!
    Sirs, I will practise on this drunken man.
    What think you, if he were conveyed to bed,
35 Wrapped in sweet clothes, rings put upon his
        fingers,
    A most delicious banquet by his bed,
    And brave attendants near him when he wakes.
    Would not the beggar then forget himself?
        First Huntsman
    Believe me, lord, I think he cannot choose.
        Second Huntsman
40 It would seem strange unto him when he waked.
        Lord
    Even as a flattering dream or worthless fancy.
    Then take him up, and manage well the jest.
    Carry him gently to my fairest chamber,
    And hang it round with all my wanton pictures;
45 Balm his foul head in warm distilled waters,
    And burn sweet wood to make the lodging sweet.
    Procure me music ready when he wakes,
    To make a dulcet and a heavenly sound.
    And if he chance to speak, be ready straight
50 And, with a low submissive reverence,
    Say 'What is it your honour will command?'
    Let one attend him with a silver basin
    Full of rose-water and bestrewed with flowers;
    Another bear the ewer, the third a diaper,
55 And say 'Will't please your lordship cool your
        hands?'
    Someone be ready with a costly suit,
    And ask him what apparel he will wear.

32 Shakespeare often refers to sleep as the
    image, or likeness, of death; compare
    Macbeth, 'Shake off this downy sleep,
    death's counterfeit' (2,3,77).

33 *practise*: play a practical joke.

35 *sweet*: scented.

36 *banquet*: In Elizabethan times, this was
    not a full meal but a selection of sweet
    dishes with fruit and wine.
37 *brave*: well-dressed.
38 *forget himself*: i.e. forget that he is a
    beggar.
39 *choose*: do anything else.

44 *wanton pictures*: The Lord probably
    means tapestry wall-hangings, depicting
    amorous scenes.
45 *Balm*: bathe
    distilled waters: e.g. rose-water, made from
    distilled rose petals.
46 *sweet wood*: e.g. juniper, or pine-cones.
48 *dulcet*: melodious.
49 *chance*: happens.
    straight: immediately.
50 *reverence*: bow.

54 *diaper*: towel.

63 *kindly*: convincingly.
64 *passing*: extremely.
65 *husbanded*: taken care of.
   with modesty: properly, without overdoing
   things.

70 *office*: appointed task.
70s.d. *Sound trumpets*: The imperative verb
   suggests that this is an instruction (not a
   description) ordering the stage-manager to
   blow the trumpet heralding the travelling
   players (see Introduction p.v).

Another tell him of his hounds and horse,
And that his lady mourns at his disease.
60 Persuade him that he hath been lunatic,
And when he says he *is*, say that he dreams,
For he is nothing but a mighty lord.
This do, and do it kindly, gentle sirs.
It will be pastime passing excellent,
65 If it be husbanded with modesty.
    First Huntsman
My Lord, I warrant you we will play our part
As he shall think by our true diligence
He is no less than what we say he is.
    Lord
Take him up gently and to bed with him,
70 And each one to his office when he wakes.

          Sly *is carried out*
          Sound trumpets

Sirrah, go see what trumpet 'tis that sounds—
                    [*Exit* Servingman
Belike some noble gentleman that means,
Travelling some journey, to repose him here.

Enter Servingman

How now? Who is it?

Servingman

75 An't please your honour, players

That offer service to your lordship.

75 *An't*: if it.

Lord

Bid them come near.

[*Enter* Players]

— Now, fellows, you are

welcome.

Players

We thank your honour.

Lord

Do you intend to stay with me tonight?

First Player

80 So please your lordship to accept our duty.

80 *So please*: if it pleases.

Lord

With all my heart. This fellow I remember

Since once he played a farmer's eldest son. —

'Twas where you wooed the gentlewoman so well.

I have forgot your name; but sure that part

85 Was aptly fitted and naturally performed.

Second Player

I think 'twas Soto that your honour means.

86 *Soto*: No extant play of this period has a
character named Soto, but it is possible
that a play now lost was revised by John
Fletcher about 1620 with the title *Women
Pleased.*

Lord

'Tis very true; thou didst it excellent.—

Well, you are come to me in happy time,

The rather for I have some sport in hand

88 *in happy time*: just at the right time.
89 *The rather*: because.
90 *cunning*: skill.

90 Wherein your cunning can assist me much.

There is a lord will hear you play tonight;

But I am doubtful of your modesties,

92 *modesties*: self-control.
93 *over-eyeing of*: staring at.
94 *yet . . . play*: he has never seen a play
before.
95 *break . . . passion*: start laughing.

Lest, over-eyeing of his odd behaviour—

For yet his honour never heard a play—

95 You break into some merry passion

And so offend him; for I tell you, sirs

If you should smile, he grows impatient.

First Player

Fear not, my lord, we can contain ourselves

Were he the veriest antic in the world.

99 *veriest*: greatest.
antic: eccentric.

Lord

[*To a* Servingman]

100 *buttery*: pantry, store-room.

100 Go, sirrah, take them to the buttery,

102 *want*: lack.
affords: can offer.

104 *suits*: respects (with a pun on 'clothes').

107 *as he will*: if he wants to.
108 *bear*: conduct.

110 *accomplishèd*: performed.

112 *low tongue*: soft voice.
lowly courtesy: humble curtsy.

115 *make known*: demonstrate.
116 *embracements*: embraces.
117-8 *With...tears*: The boy is to bend his head and cry.

120 *esteemed him*: thought himself to be.

123 *commanded tears*: tears on command.
124 *do well...shift*: be effective for that job.
125 *close conveyed*: secretly carried.
126 *in despite*: notwithstanding the natural desire (to laugh).
128 *Anon*: soon.

129 *usurp*: imitate.

132 *stay*: restrain.
133 *simple*: poor, foolish.
134 *haply*: perhaps.
135 *abate*: control.
spleen: mood; the spleen was thought to be the seat of all emotions.

And give them friendly welcome every one.
Let them want nothing that my house affords.
                      [*Exit* Servingman *with the* Players
—Sirrah, go you to Barthol'mew my page,
And see him dressed in all suits like a lady.
105 That done, conduct him to the drunkard's chamber,
And call him 'madam' — do him obeisance.
Tell him from me, as he will win my love,
He bear himself with honourable action,
Such as he hath observed in noble ladies
110 Unto their lords, by them accomplishèd.
Such duty to the drunkard let him do,
With soft low tongue and lowly courtesy,
And say 'What is't your honour will command
Wherein your lady and your humble wife
115 May show her duty and make known her love?'
And then with kind embracements, tempting kisses,
And with declining head into his bosom,
Bid him shed tears, as being overjoyed
To see her noble lord restored to health,
120 Who for this seven years hath esteemed him
No better than a poor and loathsome beggar;
And if the boy have not a woman's gift
To rain a shower of commanded tears,
An onion will do well for such a shift,
125 Which in a napkin being close conveyed,
Shall in despite enforce a watery eye.
See this dispatched with all the haste thou canst;
Anon I'll give thee more instructions.
                      [*Exit* Second Servingman
I know the boy will well usurp the grace,
130 Voice, gait, and action of a gentlewoman.
I long to hear him call the drunkard 'husband',
And how my men will stay themselves from laughter
When they do homage to this simple peasant.
I'll in to counsel them: haply my presence
135 May well abate the over-merry spleen,
Which otherwise would grow into extremes.
                                        [*Exeunt*

Induction   Scene 2

Sly has woken up, and the nobleman's servants carry out their master's orders, persuading the tinker that he is indeed a noble lord who has at last recovered from a delusion. Two life-styles are contrasted as Sly tries to learn the language and conduct appropriate for his new identity. The staging of this scene has been much debated by critics, since the direction '*Enter aloft*' seems to demand an upper gallery (which was not unusual in the Elizabethan playhouse), but the large number of characters would be too many for an ordinary balcony. But the details are of importance only for a theatrical historian: it is enough to remember the possibilities of different acting levels, which a modern director can use as desired.

1 *small ale*: the weakest (and cheapest) beer. At the beginning of the scene Sly speaks in prose, and asks for 'ale': the courtly servingmen answer in verse; and offer him 'sack'.
2 *sack*: dry white wine.
3 *conserves*: fruit preserved in sugar.
4 *raiment*: clothing.
5 *Christophero*: Sly attempts to assert himself with a Spanish version of his name.
7 *conserves of beef*: beef preserved in salt.

Scene 2

Enter aloft Sly *with* attendants (*some with apparel, basin and ewer, and other appurtenances*) *and* Lord

Sly
For God's sake, a pot of small ale.
    First Servingman
Will't please your lordship drink a cup of sack?
    Second Servingman
Will't please your honour taste of these conserves?
    Third Servingman
What raiment will your honour wear today?
    Sly
5 I am Christophero Sly, call not me 'honour' nor 'lordship'. I ne'er drank sack in my life; and if you give me any conserves, give me conserves of beef. Ne'er ask me what raiment I'll wear, for I have no more doublets than backs, no more stockings than legs, nor no more
10 shoes than feet — nay, sometime more feet than shoes, or such shoes as my toes look through the overleather.
    Lord
Heaven cease this idle humour in your honour!
O that a mighty man of such descent,

8 *doublets*: jackets, close-fitting tunics.

11 *overleather*: upper part of the shoe.
12 *idle humour*: foolish mood.
13 *descent*: noble birth.
14 *esteem*: reputation.
15 *infusèd*: possessed.
16 *would you*: do you want to.
17 *Burton-heath*: Barton-on-the-Heath, a village about 15 miles from Shakespeare's birthplace, Stratford-upon-Avon.
18 *cardmaker*: maker of 'cards' — toothed instruments for combing wool, much needed in the wool-producing area around Stratford.
   transmutation: changing his job.
   bear-herd: keeper of a performing bear.
20 *ale-wife*: woman who keeps an ale-house.
   Wincot: The small hamlet of Wincot, in the parish of Quinton, was four miles south of Stratford; the daughter of Robert Hacket was baptized there in 1591.
21 *on the score*: in debt; alehouse debts were chalked up on a board for all to see.
22 *sheer ale*: just for ale.
   score: mark.
23 *Christendom*: the Christian world.
   bestraught: mad, out of my mind.
   Here's ––: Sly is trying to offer proof of his identity, but he can find none.
27 *As*: as though.
29 *ancient*: former.
32 *beck*: nod.
33 *Apollo*: the classical god of music; the Servingmen are striving for a courtly effect.
36 *lustful*: enticing.
37 *trimmed up*: dressed up.
   Semiramis: a legendary queen of Assyria, renowned for amorous encounters.
38 *bestrew*: spread rushes (probably) as a carpet.

Of such possessions, and so high esteem,
15 Should be infusèd with so foul a spirit!

Sly
What, would you make me mad? Am not I Christopher Sly, old Sly's son of Burton-heath, by birth a pedlar, by education a cardmaker, by transmutation a bear-herd, and now by present profession a tinker? Ask
20 Marian Hacket, the fat ale-wife of Wincot, if she know me not: if she say I am not fourteen pence on the score for sheer ale, score me up for the lyingest knave in Christendom. What! I am not bestraught. Here's —

Third Servingman
O, this it is that makes your lady mourn.

Second Servingman
25 O, this is it that makes your servants droop.

Lord
Hence comes it that your kindred shuns your house
As beaten hence by your strange lunacy.
O noble lord, bethink thee of thy birth,
Call home thy ancient thoughts from banishment,
30 And banish hence these abject lowly dreams.
Look how thy servants do attend on thee,
Each in his office ready at thy beck.
Wilt thou have music? [*Music*] Hark, Apollo plays,
And twenty cagèd nightingales do sing.
35 Or wilt thou sleep? We'll have thee to a couch
Softer and sweeter than the lustful bed
On purpose trimmed up for Semiramis.
Say thou wilt walk; we will bestrew the ground.
Or wilt thou ride? Thy horses shall be trapped,
40 Their harness studded all with gold and pearl.
Dost thou love hawking? Thou hast hawks will soar
Above the morning lark. Or wilt thou hunt?
Thy hounds shall make the welkin answer them
And fetch shrill echoes from the hollow earth.

First Servingman
45 Say thou wilt course, thy greyhounds are as swift
As breathèd stags — ay, fleeter than the roe.

Second Servingman
Dost thou love pictures? We will fetch thee straight
Adonis painted by a running brook,
And Cytherea all in sedges hid,
50 Which seem to move and wanton with her breath,
Even as the waving sedges play with wind.

39 *trapped*: caparisoned, draped in protective, decorative, coverings.

43–4 The Elizabethans prized their hounds for the musical sound of their baying when in pursuit of the quarry.

43 *welkin*: sky — a 'poetic' word.

45 *course*: chase the hare, hunting by sight not scent.

46 *breathèd*: strong-winded.
fleeter: faster.
roe: a small deer.

47 *straight*: immediately.

48–58 These paintings (the 'wanton pictures' ordered by the Lord in Scene 1) illustrate some of the stories in Ovid's *Metamorphoses*. Adonis was a handsome human boy who was loved by Venus — Cytherea — the goddess of love; Shakespeare narrates this fable in his poem *Venus and Adonis*. The god Zeus fell in love with the virgin Io, and hid in a cloud to seduce her; afterwards she was turned into a heifer. Daphne tried to escape from the attentions of the god Apollo, and was changed into a laurel tree.

49 *sedges*: rushes.

54 *lively*: life-like.
as . . . done: as though the deed were just being done.

58 *workmanly*: skilfully.

59 *nothing but*: no less than.

60 *a lady*: The descriptions of these 'wanton pictures', with their 'lively' representation of sexual encounters, leads up to the promise of a real 'woman' for Sly.

61 *this waning age*: this modern world (with an allusion to the classical belief that the world was declining from the original Golden Age — which could be interpreted as the Bible's Garden of Eden).

62 *till*: until, before.

63 *envious*: malicious.
o'errun: flowed over.

65 *yet*: even now.

66–73 Sly, persuaded that he is indeed a lord, begins to speak in verse — which Elizabethan dramatic decorum prescribed for the more noble characters. He speaks to himself as he tests his five senses (to prove that he is not dreaming), then addresses the servingmen grandly when he demands 'our lady' — but betrays himself when he calls for 'a pot o'th'smallest ale'.

Lord
We'll show thee Io as she was a maid,
And how she was beguilèd and surprised,
As lively painted as the deed was done.

Third Servingman
55 Or Daphne roaming through a thorny wood,
Scratching her legs that one shall swear she bleeds,
And at that sight shall sad Apollo weep,
So workmanly the blood and tears are drawn.

Lord
Thou art a lord, and nothing but a lord.
60 Thou hast a lady far more beautiful
Than any woman in this waning age.

First Servingman
And till the tears that she hath shed for thee
Like envious floods o'errun her lovely face
She was the fairest creature in the world,
65 And yet she is inferior to none.

Sly
Am I a lord, and have I such a lady?
Or do I dream? Or have I dreamed till now?
I do not sleep: I see, I hear, I speak,
I smell sweet savours and I feel soft things.
70 Upon my life, I am a lord indeed,
And not a tinker nor Christopher Sly.
Well, bring our lady hither to our sight,
And once again a pot o'th' smallest ale.

Second Servingman
Will't please your mightiness to wash your hands?
75 O how we joy to see your wit restored,
O that once more you knew but what you are!
These fifteen years you have been in a dream,
Or when you waked, so waked as if you slept.

Sly
These fifteen years! By my fay, a goodly nap.
80 But did I never speak of all that time?

First Servingman
Oh yes, my lord, but very idle words,
For though you lay here in this goodly chamber,
Yet would you say ye were beaten out of door,
And rail upon the hostess of the house,
85 And say you would present her at the leet
Because she brought stone jugs and no sealed quarts.
Sometimes you would call out for Cicely Hacket.

75 *joy*: rejoice.
   wit: sense.
77 *fifteen*: The servingman increases the
   Lord's time.
79 *fay*: faith.
80 *of*: during.
81 *idle*: silly.
82 *goodly*: fine.
83 *out of door*: out of the house.
84 *rail upon*: shout about.
85 *present . . . leet*: take her to court (for
   giving short measure).
86 *stone . . . quarts*: The quart measures
   were officially stamped to guarantee
   capacity, but the earthenware jugs were
   unmarked — and commonly used by
   dishonest innkeepers.
87 *Cicely Hacket*: see *note* to *Induction*, 2,20.
88 *the . . . house*: the landlady's daughter.
90 *reckoned up*: referred to.
91-2 These might have been the names of
   real people — and a director could
   substitute the names of local personalities.
   Greece: This may be an error; perhaps
   Shakespeare wrote 'Greete' — the name of
   a village near Stratford.
95 *amends*: improvement.
97 *I thank thee*: Sly acknowledges the drink
   he has been given.
   thou . . . it: i.e. 'I'll pay you later.'
98 *How fares*: how is. The Page is enquiring
   about the 'lord's' health; but Sly in the
   next line makes a pun on 'fare' = take
   nourishment.
99 *cheer*: nourishment.
103 *goodman*: The peasant's word for
   'husband'.

105 *in all obedience*: In the old form of the
   Marriage Service, the woman promised to
   'love, honour, and obey' her husband.

Sly
Ay, the woman's maid of the house.
   Third Servingman
Why, sir, you know no house, nor no such maid,
90 Nor no such men as you have reckoned up —
As Stephen Sly, and old John Naps of Greece,
And Peter Turf, and Henry Pimpernel,
And twenty more such names and men as these,
Which never were nor no man ever saw.
   Sly
95 Now Lord be thanked for my good amends.
   All
Amen.

Enter Page *dressed as a lady, with*
attendants; one hands Sly a pot of ale.

   Sly
I thank thee, thou shalt not lose by it.
   Page
How fares my noble lord?
   Sly
Marry, I fare well, for here is cheer enough.
100 Where is my wife?
   Page
Here, noble lord; what is thy will with her?
   Sly
Are you my wife, and will not call me 'husband'?
My men should call me 'lord'; I am your goodman.
   Page
My husband and my lord, my lord and husband,
105 I am your wife in all obedience.
   Sly
I know it well. — What must I call her?
   Lord
'Madam'.
   Sly
'Alice madam', or 'Joan madam'?
   Lord
'Madam', and nothing else, so lords call ladies.
   Sly
110 Madam wife, they say that I have dreamed
And slept for above some fifteen year or more.

Page
Ay, and the time seems thirty unto me,
Being all this time abandoned from your bed.

Sly
'Tis much. Servants, leave me and her alone.

[*Exeunt* Lord *and* Servingmen

115 Madam, undress you and come now to bed.

Page
Thrice-noble lord, let me entreat of you
To pardon me yet for a night or two,
Or, if not so, until the sun be set,
For your physicians have expressly charged,

120 In peril to incur your former malady,
That I should yet absent me from your bed.
I hope this reason stands for my excuse.

Sly
Ay, it stands so that I may hardly tarry so long! But
I would be loath to fall into my dreams again; I will

125 therefore tarry in despite of the flesh and the blood.

Enter a Servingman

Servingman
Your honour's players, hearing your amendment,
Are come to play a pleasant comedy;
For so your doctors hold it very meet,
Seeing too much sadness hath congealed your blood,

130 And melancholy is the nurse of frenzy,
Therefore they thought it good you hear a play
And frame your mind to mirth and merriment,
Which bars a thousand harms, and lengthens life.

Sly
Marry, I will. Let them play it. Is not a comonty a

135 Christmas gambol or a tumbling-trick?

Page
No, my good lord, it is more pleasing stuff.

Sly
What, household stuff?

Page
It is a kind of history.

Sly
Well, we'll see't. Come madam wife, sit by my side

140 and let the world slip; we shall ne'er be younger.

---

113   *abandoned*: banished.

117   *pardon*: excuse.

119   *expressly charged*: especially ordered.
120   *In peril*: at the risk of.

123   *it stands*: Sly is aroused — and he forgets the formal verse in his sexual innuendoes. *hardly*: with difficulty. *tarry*: hold back, wait.

128   *hold it very meet*: think it is a very good idea.
129–30   Elizabethan medical theory taught that melancholy caused a thickening of the blood, and this in its turn was the cause ('nurse') of madness ('frenzy').
132   *frame*: suit.
133   *bars*: prevents.

134   *comonty*: The word 'comedy' is new to Sly.
135   *gambol*: game. *tumbling-trick*: acrobatics.

137   *household stuff*: homely fun.

138   *history*: story, narrative.

140   *let . . . younger*: i.e. let us enjoy ourselves.

Act I

Act I Scene I

The play proper begins when the trumpets herald the arrival of Lucentio, who proceeds to explain to his manservant, Tranio, where they are, why they have come, and where they have come from. This is a conventional technique for making sure that the audience is in possession of some necessary facts. The exposition is interrupted, however, by a family quarrel. Lucentio and Tranio stand aside to witness the problems of a father with two daughters — one of whom is the 'shrew', Katherina, whom no man will marry; the other is the fair Bianca, beloved of Gremio and Hortensio. The father, Baptista, decrees that none shall have the younger until a husband is found for the elder. Bianca's two lovers agree to forget their rivalry and join forces to find a husband for Katherina. The watching Lucentio has also fallen in love, and he exchanges clothes with Tranio so that, disguised, he can present himself as a tutor and so gain access to Bianca. When Biondello, Lucentio's servant, arrives from Pisa, he is taken into the secret.

1 *since for*: because of.
2 *Padua*: Padua was famous for its ancient university, which was founded in 1228 and was a great centre ('nursery') for all branches of learning ('arts').

Scene I

A flourish. Enter Lucentio *and his man* Tranio

Lucentio
Tranio, since for the great desire I had
To see fair Padua, nursery of arts,
I am arrived for fruitful Lombardy,
The pleasant garden of great Italy,
5   And by my father's love and leave am armed
With his good will and thy good company,
My trusty servant well approved in all,
Here let us breathe and haply institute
A course of learning and ingenious studies.
10 Pisa renowned for grave citizens
Gave me my being, and my father first,
A merchant of great traffic through the world,
Vincentio, come of the Bentivolii.
Vincentio's son, brought up in Florence,
15 It shall become to serve all hopes conceived
To deck his fortune with his virtuous deeds;
And therefore, Tranio, for the time I study
Virtue, and that part of philosophy
Will I apply that treats of happiness
20 By virtue specially to be achieved.

3 *am arrived*: have arrived; the auxiliary 'be'
was often used (as in modern French)
with verbs of motion.
for: in.
fruitful Lombardy: In some sixteenth-
century maps — such as that of Ortelius
— LOMBARDY was marked across the
whole of north Italy; the region was
commonly known as the garden of Italy.
5 *leave*: permission.
7 *well approved in all*: shown by experience
to be good in every way.
8 *breathe*: pause, have a rest.
haply: maybe
institute: begin.
9 *ingenious*: intellectual.
10 *renowned*: famous; the line is repeated at
4, 2, 97.
11 *Gave . . . being*: was my birthplace.
first: before me.
12 *great . . . world*: involved in major
international enterprises.
13 *come of*: descended from.
the Bentivolii: A famous Italian family —
of Bologna, not Pisa.
14-16 It is only right that Vincentio's son,
brought up in Florence, should fulfil the
hopes that people have had for him by
adding great deeds to the fortunes he has
inherited.
17 *for the time*: at present.
19 *apply*: concentrate on.
treats of: deals with.
19-20 Aristotle's *Ethics 1* and *2* develops the
idea that happiness can only be achieved
through virtuous living.
21 *thy mind*: what you think of it.
22 *as he that*: like a man who.
23 *plash*: pool.
24 *with satiety*: by having too much.
25 *Mi pardonato*: excuse me; this, and other
Italian phrases in the first act, serve to
persuade the audience that Elizabethan
Warwickshire has given place to
Renaissance Italy.
26 'I feel just the same as you do about it
all.'
27 *resolve*: determination.
28 *suck the sweets*: Tranio's metaphor is of
the bee taking nectar from the flower.
31 *stoics . . . stocks*: The pun did not
originate with Tranio; 'stoics' endure
everything, and 'stocks' appreciate
nothing.

Tell me thy mind; for I have Pisa left
And am to Padua come as he that leaves
A shallow plash to plunge him in the deep,
And with satiety seeks to quench his thirst.

Tranio

25 *Me pardonato*, gentle master mine:
I am in all affected as yourself,
Glad that you thus continue your resolve
To suck the sweets of sweet philosophy;
Only, good master, while we do admire
30 This virtue and this moral discipline,
Let's be no stoics, nor no stocks, I pray,
Or so devote to Aristotle's checks
As Ovid be an outcast quite abjured.
Balk logic with acquaintance that you have,
35 And practise rhetoric in your common talk;
Music and poesy use to quicken you;
The mathematics and the metaphysics
Fall to them as you find your stomach serves you.
No profit grows where is no pleasure ta'en.
40 In brief, sir, study what you most affect.

Lucentio

Gramercies, Tranio, well dost thou advise.
If, Biondello, thou wert come ashore,
We could at once put us in readiness,
And take a lodging fit to entertain
45 Such friends as time in Padua shall beget.
But stay awhile, what company is this?

Tranio

Master, some show to welcome us to town.

Enter Baptista *with his two daughters*
Katherina *and* Bianca; Gremio, *a
pantaloon; and* Hortensio, *suitor to* Bianca.
Lucentio *and* Tranio *stand by.*

Baptista

Gentlemen, importune me no farther,
For how I firmly am resolved you know:
50 That is, not to bestow my youngest daughter
Before I have a husband for the elder.
If either of you both love Katherina,
Because I know you well, and love you well,
Leave shall you have to court her at your pleasure.

32 *devote*: devoted.
Aristotle's checks: the Greek philosopher's counsels of moderation.
33 *Ovid*: A Roman poet, popular among the Elizabethans for his erotic verse narratives; he was literally an 'outcast' during his lifetime, when he was exiled from Rome.
abjured: forsworn, renounced.
34 *Balk logic*: engage in arguments.
acquaintance: friends.
35 *rhetoric*: the art of communication; this was one of the academic disciplines, like logic and mathematics.
36 *use*: make use of.
quicken: refresh.
38 'Eat of them when you have the appetite.'
40 *most affect*: like best.
41 *Gramercies*: many thanks.
42 *come ashore*: Padua is not a sea-port; but Shakespeare probably knew of the network of inland waterways that linked the cities of northern Italy.
43 *put . . . readiness*: get started.
47 *show*: entertainment.
47s.d. Such detailed stage directions were probably written by Shakespeare himself.
pantaloon: foolish old man (a stock figure in the Italian *commedia dell'arte*, whose function was usually to act as an obstacle to the young lovers).
48 *importune . . . further*: don't go on asking me.
50 *bestow*: give in marriage.
youngest: younger (the superlative form was often used when only two objects were compared).
54 *Leave*: permission.
55 *cart*: Gremio makes a pun on 'court'; convicted prostitutes were punished by being whipped as they were drawn through the streets at the tail of a cart.
rough: violent.
56 *will you*: do you want.
58 *make . . . mates*: make me a laughing-stock for these fellows. A 'stale' is also a decoy: she is being used to trap husbands — 'mates' — for her sister; and a prostitute. In the game of chess, 'stalemate' is the final position before the game is lost.
60 *mould*: nature.

Gremio

55 To cart her rather. She's too rough for me.
There, there Hortensio, will you any wife?

Katherina

[*To* Baptista]
I pray you, sir, is it your will
To make a stale of me amongst these mates?

Hortensio

'Mates', maid, how mean you that? No mates for you
60 Unless you were of gentler, milder mould.

Katherina

I'faith, sir, you shall never need to fear;
Iwis it is not halfway to her heart.
But if it were, doubt not her care should be
To comb your noddle with a three-legged stool,
65 And paint your face, and use you like a fool.

Hortensio

From all such devils, good Lord deliver us!

Gremio

And me too, good Lord!

Tranio

[*Aside to* Lucentio]
Husht, master, here's some good pastime toward;
That wench is stark mad, or wonderful froward.

Lucentio

[*Aside to Tranio*]
70 But in the other's silence do I see
Maid's mild behaviour and sobriety.
Peace, Tranio.

Tranio

[*Aside to Lucentio*]
Well said, master. Mum! and gaze your fill.

Baptista

Gentlemen, that I may soon make good
75 What I have said — Bianca, get you in,
And let it not displease thee, good Bianca,
For I will love thee ne'er the less, my girl.

Katherina

A pretty peat! It is best
Put finger in the eye, an she knew why.

62 *Iwis*: indeed.
   it . . . heart: (i.e. marriage) is not something she cares about (Katherina speaks of herself).
63 *doubt not*: i.e. I promise you.
64 *comb your noddle*: hit your silly head.
65 *paint your face*: i.e. with your own blood.
66 *From . . . us*: Hortensio paraphrases a line from the Church of England Litany: 'from the crafts and assaults of the devil . . . Good Lord, deliver us'.
68 *toward*: about to happen.
69 *froward*: bad-tempered.
71 *sobriety*: modesty.
73 *Mum*: keep quiet.
74 *make good*: accomplish.
75 *in*: indoors.
78 *peat*: little pet.
   It is best: you ought to.
79 *finger in the eye*: i.e. to bring tears.
   an . . . why: if she had any sense.
80 *content . . . discontent*: be satisfied now that I am unhappy.
81 *pleasure*: will.
   subscribe: obey.
84 *Minerva*: the Roman goddess of wisdom.
85 *strange*: unfriendly.
86 *effects*: causes.
87 *mew her up*: lock her up — as a falcon is confined in a mew during its moulting season.
88 *for*: because of.
89 'Make Bianca suffer for what Katherina has said.'
90 *content ye*: you must be satisfied.
   am resolved: have made my mind up.
92 *for*: because.
97 *Prefer them hither*: introduce me to them.
   cunning: skilful.
98 *liberal*: generous.
99 *bringing-up*: education.
101 *commune*: discuss.
105-8 Gremio seems to be uttering some proverbial wisdom — although no parallels have been found.
105 *the devil's dam*: the devil's mother — said to be worse than the devil himself.
   gifts: qualities.
106 *hold*: detain.
   Their love . . . great: loving women is not so very important.
107 *blow our nails*: wait patiently.

Bianca

80 Sister, content you in my discontent.
—Sir, to your pleasure humbly I subscribe:
My books and instruments shall be my company,
On them to look and practise by myself.

Lucentio

[*Aside to* Tranio]
Hark, Tranio, thou mayst hear Minerva speak.

Hortensio

85 Signor Baptista, will you be so strange?
Sorry I am that our good will effects
   Bianca's grief.

Gremio

Why will you mew her up,
Signor Baptista, for this fiend of hell,
And make her bear the penance of her tongue?

Baptista

90 Gentlemen, content ye. I am resolved.
Go in, Bianca.   [*Exit* Bianca
And for I know she taketh most delight
In music, instruments, and poetry,
Schoolmasters will I keep within my house
95 Fit to instruct her youth. If you, Hortensio,
Or Signor Gremio, you, know any such,
Prefer them hither; for to cunning men
I will be very kind, and liberal
To mine own children in good bringing-up.
100 And so farewell. — Katherina, you may stay,
For I have more to commune with Bianca.   [*Exit*

Katherina

Why, and I trust I may go too, may I not? What, shall I
be appointed hours, as though, belike, I knew not what
to take and what to leave? Ha!   [*Exit*

Gremio

105 You may go to the devil's dam: your gifts are so good
here's none will hold you. — Their love is not so great,
Hortensio, but we may blow our nails together, and
fast it fairly out. Our cake's dough on both sides.
Farewell. Yet, for the love I bear my sweet Bianca,
110 if I can by any means light on a fit man to teach her
that wherein she delights, I will wish him to her father.

Hortensio

So will I, Signor Gremio; but a word, I pray. Though

108 *fast it fairly out*: manage to survive.
   Our . . . sides: it's the same for both of
   us.
110 *light on*: find.
111 *wish*: recommend.
113 *brooked parley*: allowed us to talk to each
   other.
114 *upon advice*: on consideration.
   toucheth: concerns.
116 *to labour and effect*: to get to work and
   achieve.
119 *Marry*: by (the Virgin) Mary (a mild
   oath).
123 *so very a fool*: such a complete fool.

126 *alarums*: war-cries (literally, the trumpet-
   calls to battle).
127 *an*: if.
128 *and money enough*: if there's enough
   money.
129 *I cannot tell*: I don't know about that.
   as lief: just as soon.
130 *the high cross*: the market cross, in the
   middle of the town.

132 *small . . . apples*: not much to choose
   between the two evils; in their use of
   clichés, there seems to be 'small choice'
   between the commonplace minds of
   Hortensio and Gremio.
133 *bar in law*: legal obstacle — Baptista has a
   parent's legal right to prohibit Bianca's
   marriage.

the nature of our quarrel yet never brooked parley, know now, upon advice, it toucheth us both, that we may yet again have access to our fair mistress and be happy rivals in Bianca's love—, to labour and effect one thing specially.

Gremio
What's that, I pray?

Hortensio
Marry, sir, to get a husband for her sister.

Gremio
A husband? A devil.

Hortensio
I say a husband.

Gremio
I say a devil. Think'st thou, Hortensio, though her father be very rich, any man is so very a fool to be married to hell?

Hortensio
Tush, Gremio; though it pass your patience and mine to endure her loud alarums, why, man, there be good fellows in the world, an a man could light on them, would take her with all faults, and money enough.

Gremio
I cannot tell; but I had as lief take her dowry with this condition — to be whipped at the high cross every morning.

Hortensio
Faith, as you say, there's small choice in rotten apples. But come, since this bar in law makes us friends, it shall be so far forth friendly maintained till by helping Baptista's eldest daughter to a husband we set his youngest free for a husband, and then have to't afresh.

134 *so . . . maintained*: let us keep up the friendship to a certain extent.

136 *have to't*: on with the fight (their rivalry).

137 *Happy . . . dole*: he's a lucky man that gets her.

he . . . fastest: In medieval jousting, 'tilting for the ring' was part of the sport; the winner carried off the ring with his lance.

139 *am agreed*: agree with you.

him: any man.

141 *woo . . . bed her*: A commonplace description of love's progress.

rid . . . her: Gremio has something of his own to add.

148 'I fell in love.' Idleness and amorousness are commonly associated by poetic writers, and the pansy, sometimes called 'heartsease' or 'love-in-idleness', was thought to have magic powers as an aphrodisiac.

149 *in plainness*: in all honesty.

150 *secret*: trustworthy, able to keep secrets.

151 *Anna . . . Carthage*: In his play *Dido Queen of Carthage* Christopher Marlowe (Shakespeare's greatest contemporary) showed Anna as the trusted confidante of her sister Dido, whose story is told in Virgil's *Aeneid*, Book IV. Lucentio's sudden passion seems almost like an imitation of Dido, who burnt herself to death when Aeneas deserted her.

153 *achieve*: secure as a wife.

157 *is not . . . heart*: cannot be driven out of the heart by scolding.

158 *naught . . . so*: all you can do is this.

159 'Now that you have been caught, buy yourself out as cheaply as you can.' The quotation (originally from a play by Terence) comes in Lily's *Latin Grammar*, the textbook used in Shakespeare's school.

160 *Gramercies*: thanks very much.

this contents: I like your advice.

162 *longly*: for such a long time.

163 *marked . . . all*: didn't see what is really going on; in classical comedy it is often the function of the servant to explain the plot to his love-sick master.

165 *daughter of Agenor*: Europa, who was carried away from her father's kingdom by Jupiter (Jove) disguised as a bull. The lover's rhapsody seems to mistake the

Sweet Bianca! Happy man be his dole: he that runs fastest gets the ring. How say you, Signor Gremio?

Gremio

I am agreed, and would I had given him the best horse
140 in Padua to begin his wooing that would thoroughly woo her, wed her, and bed her, and rid the house of her. Come on.

[*Exeunt* Gremio *and* Hortensio

Tranio

I pray, sir, tell me, is it possible
That love should of a sudden take such hold?

Lucentio

145 O Tranio, till I found it to be true,
I never thought it possible or likely.
But see, while idly I stood looking on,
I found the effect of love-in-idleness,
And now in plainness do confess to thee,
150 That art to me as secret and as dear
As Anna to the Queen of Carthage was,
Tranio, I burn, I pine, I perish, Tranio,
If I achieve not this young modest girl.
Counsel me, Tranio, for I know thou canst;
155 Assist me, Tranio, for I know thou wilt.

Tranio

Master, it is no time to chide you now;
Affection is not rated from the heart.
If love have touched you, naught remains but so:
Redime te captam quam queas minimo.

Lucentio

160 Gramercies, lad. Go forward, this contents;
The rest will comfort, for thy counsel's sound.

Tranio

Master, you looked so longly on the maid,
Perhaps you marked not what's the pith of all.

Lucentio

O yes, I saw sweet beauty in her face,
165 Such as the daughter of Agenor had,
That made great Jove to humble him to her hand,
When with his knees he kissed the Cretan strand.

Tranio

Saw you no more? Marked you not how her sister
Began to scold and raise up such a storm
170 That mortal ears might hardly endure the din?

story slightly: Jupiter courted Europa in Tyre, before abducting her to Crete.

170   *hardly*: scarcely.

177   *curst and shrewd*: bad-tempered and sharp-tongued.

180   *mewed her up*: confined her; compare line 87 *note*.
181   *because*: so that.

183   *art . . . advised*: didn't you notice.
184   *cunning*: skilful; but Lucentio's meaning almost embraces the modern (= crafty) sense of the word.
185   *'tis plotted*: I have a plan.

186   *for my hand*: at a guess.
187   *inventions*: schemes.
      jump in one: coincide.

190   *device*: plan.
      May it be done?: will it work?

191   *bear your part*: take your place.

193   *ply*: work at.

195   *Basta*: enough; Shakespeare remembers the Italian setting of the plot.
      full: all worked out.

Lucentio
Tranio, I saw her coral lips to move,
And with her breath she did perfume the air.
Sacred and sweet was all I saw in her.
    Tranio
Nay, then 'tis time to stir him from his trance.
175   I pray, awake sir. If you love the maid,
Bend thoughts and wits to achieve her. Thus it stands:
Her elder sister is so curst and shrewd
That till the father rid his hands of her,
Master, your love must live a maid at home,
180   And therefore has he closely mewed her up,
Because she will not be annoyed with suitors.
    Lucentio
Ah Tranio, what a cruel father's he!
But art thou not advised he took some care
To get her cunning schoolmasters to instruct her?
    Tranio
185   Ay, marry, am I, sir — and now 'tis plotted.
    Lucentio
I have it, Tranio.
    Tranio   Master, for my hand,
Both our inventions meet and jump in one.
    Lucentio
Tell me thine first.
    Tranio   You will be schoolmaster,
And undertake the teaching of the maid:
190   That's your device.
    Lucentio   It is. May it be done?
    Tranio
Not possible: for who shall bear your part
And be in Padua here Vincentio's son,
Keep house and ply his book, welcome his friends,
Visit his countrymen and banquet them?
    Lucentio
195   *Basta*, content thee, for I have it full.
We have not yet been seen in any house,
Nor can we be distinguished by our faces
For man or master. Then it follows thus:
Thou shalt be master, Tranio, in my stead,
200   Keep house, and port, and servants, as I should;

202 *meaner*: humbler (i.e. than Lucentio himself).
204 *Uncase*: undress.
    coloured: Elizabethan servants were soberly dressed; the coloured clothes were worn by their masters.
206 *charm*: make him promise.

207 'You will need to.'
208 *sith*: since.
209 *tied*: bound.
210 *at our parting*: when we left.
211 *be serviceable*: do your best to serve.

I will some other be — some Florentine,
Some Neapolitan, or meaner man of Pisa.
'Tis hatched, and shall be so. Tranio, at once
Uncase thee; take my coloured hat and cloak.
205 When Biondello comes, he waits on thee,
But I will charm him first to keep his tongue.

Tranio
So had you need.
In brief, sir, sith it your pleasure is,
And I am tied to be obedient —
210 For so your father charged me at our parting:
'Be serviceable to my son', quoth he,
Although I think 'twas in another sense—
I am content to be Lucentio,
Because so well I love Lucentio.

They exchange clothes

Lucentio
215 Tranio, be so, because Lucentio loves,
And let me be a slave t'achieve that maid
Whose sudden sight hath thralled my wounded eye.

217 *thralled*: enslaved.
    wounded eye: Cupid's arrow, inducing love, wounded Lucentio in the eye when he saw Bianca.

Enter Biondello

Here comes the rogue. Sirrah, where have you been?
Biondello
Where have I been? Nay, how now, where are you?
220 Master, has my fellow Tranio stolen your clothes, or you stolen his, or both? Pray, what's the news?

221 *what's the news*: what's going on.

Lucentio
Sirrah, come hither. 'Tis no time to jest,
And therefore frame your manners to the time.
Your fellow Tranio here, to save my life,

223 *frame*: fit.

225 Puts my apparel and my countenance on,
And I for my escape have put on his;
For in a quarrel since I came ashore
I killed a man, and fear I was descried.
Wait you on him, I charge you, as becomes,
230 While I make way from hence to save my life;
You understand me?

225 *countenance*: identity.

227-8 This seems unnecessary; Lucentio is over-enthusiastic about his plot.
228 *descried*: seen.
229 *as becomes*: in the proper way.

Biondello
I, sir? Ne'er a whit.

232 *Ne'er a whit*: not at all.

233 'Not a word about Tranio.'

236–41 A doggerel verse marks Tranio's change from servant to master.

239 *use your manners*: behave yourself.

242 *rests*: remains.
that thyself execute: which you must carry out.
244 *sufficeth*: let it be enough for you to know.

245s.d. *Presenters*: commentators (actors playing the parts of spectators).

246 *nod*: fall asleep.
mind: pay attention to.

247 *Saint Anne*: mother of the Virgin Mary.
matter: subject.

251s.d. *sit and mark*: The stage direction seems to indicate that the 'presenters' remain in their positions for the rest of the play, but Shakespeare seems to forget about them: they never speak again in *The Taming of the Shrew*. See Appendix A, p.101.

Lucentio
And not a jot of Tranio in your mouth.
Tranio is changed into Lucentio.
Biondello
235 The better for him. Would I were so too!
Tranio
So would I, 'faith, boy, to have the next wish after,
That Lucentio indeed had Baptista's youngest daughter.
But sirrah, not for my sake but your master's, I advise
You use your manners discreetly in all kind of companies.
240 When I am alone, why then I am Tranio.
But in all places else your master Lucentio.
Lucentio
Tranio, let's go. One thing more rests, that thyself execute, to make one among these wooers. If thou ask me why, sufficeth my reasons are both good and
245 weighty.
[*Exeunt*

The Presenters *above speak*

Servingman
My lord, you nod, you do not mind the play.
Sly
Yes, by Saint Anne, do I. A good matter, surely; comes there any more of it?
Page (*As lady*)
My lord, 'tis but begun.
Sly
250 'Tis a very excellent piece of work, madam lady: would 'twere done!

They sit and mark

Act 1 Scene 2

Petruchio and his servant Grumio have arrived in Padua; we are told a little about Petruchio's circumstances — and shown something of his temper. He declares his intention of finding a rich wife for himself, and when Hortensio describes Katherina, Petruchio happily accepts the challenge. Grumio, the servant, adds his own comments on his master. Hortensio confides in Petruchio, and tells of his plan to gain access to Bianca. His rival Gremio, meanwhile, has found another teacher for Bianca — and this is Lucentio, disguised as Tranio and calling himself by his servant's name. Petruchio is introduced as the man who is willing to marry Katherina and thereby free Bianca so that one of her lovers can get her hand in marriage. The real Tranio, calling himself Lucentio, enters to announce his determination to court Bianca, and agrees to share with Hortensio and Gremio in paying Petruchio to marry Katherina.

2 *of all*: most of all.
3 *approvèd*: trusted.
4 *trow*: believe.
   this is his house: The Elizabethan stage had two doors at the back; Petruchio could enter at one door, coming into Padua, and cross to the other, finding Hortensio's 'house'. See Illustration p.7.
6–7 *Knock . . . rebused*: Grumio misunderstands Petruchio's words, and confuses his own; 'knock' was commonly used as 'beat', but 'rebused' is Grumio's own muddle of 'abused' and 'rebuked'.
8 *me*: for me.
12 *rap me well*: knock loudly for me.
   knave's pate: fool of a head. The doggerel rhyming verse is appropriate for slapstick comedy.
14 'You want me to hit you first' — so Grumio would give Petruchio reason to beat his servant.
15 *comes by*: suffers.
16 Petruchio is exasperated.
17 *an*: if.
   ring it: i.e. the bell — with a pun on 'wring'.
18 *solfa*: sing a musical scale; the verb from 'solfa' is Shakespeare's own coinage.
22 *How do you all*: how is everybody.
24 *fray*: fighting.

Scene 2

Enter Petruchio *and his man* Grumio

Petruchio
Verona, for a while I take my leave,
To see my friends in Padua, but of all
My best belovèd and approvèd friend,
Hortensio; and I trow this is his house.
5 Here, sirrah Grumio, knock, I say.
Grumio
Knock, sir? Whom should I knock? Is there any man
has rebused your worship?
Petruchio
Villain, I say, knock me here soundly.
Grumio
Knock you here, sir? Why, sir, what am I, sir, that I
10 should knock you here, sir?
Petruchio
Villain, I say, knock me at this gate,
And rap me well, or I'll knock your knave's pate.
Grumio
My master is grown quarrelsome.
I should knock you first,
15 And then I know after who comes by the worst.
Petruchio
Will it not be?
Faith, sirrah, an you'll not knock, I'll ring it;
I'll try how you can solfa and sing it,

He wrings him by the ears

Grumio
Help, masters, help, my master is mad!
Petruchio
20 Now knock when I bid you, sirrah villain.

Enter Hortensio

Hortensio
How now, what's the matter? My old friend Grumio,
and my good friend Petruchio? How do you all at
Verona?
Petruchio
Signor Hortensio, come you to part the fray?
25 *Con tutto il cuore ben trovato*, may I say.

25 'With all my heart, it's good to meet
    you.'
26 'Welcome to our house, most honoured
    Petruchio.'
27 *compound*: settle.
29 *'leges*: alleges; Grumio is an English
    servant in his mistrust of foreign
    languages, mistaking Italian for Latin.
33 *two . . . out*: Grumio implies that
    Petruchio is slightly mad — perhaps
    drunk. He alludes to the card game 'One
    and thirty' (in French, *trente et un*),
    where the player must collect cards
    whose spots (pips) amount to 31 exactly;
    to score 32 was excessive. Perhaps, also,
    Grumio refers to his master's age.

38 *for my heart*: for my life.
41 *come you now*: are you now saying.
43 *advise*: warn.
44 *pledge*: surety.
45 *this*: this is.
    a heavy chance: a bad business.
46 *pleasant*: merry.
47 *happy*: fortunate.
49 *Such*: the same.
50 *farther . . . home*: away from home.
51 *Where . . . grows*: where there's not much
    opportunity.
    in a few: briefly.
52 *thus it stands*: it's like this.
54 *thrust . . . maze*: i.e. come out into the
    confused paths of this world.
55 *Happily*: with any luck.
    to wive . . . may: get married and do as
    well as I can for myself.

Hortensio

*Alla nostra casa ben venuto, molto honorata signor mio
Petruchio.* — Rise, Grumio, rise. We will compound
this quarrel.

Grumio

Nay, 'tis no matter, sir, what he 'leges in Latin.
30 If this be not a lawful cause for me to leave his service!
Look you, sir: he bid me knock him, and rap him
soundly, sir. Well, was it fit for a servant to use his
master so, being perhaps, for aught I see, two and
thirty, a pip out? Whom would to God I had well
35 knocked at first. Then had not Grumio come by the
worst.

Petruchio

A senseless villain. Good Hortensio,
I bade the rascal knock upon your gate,
And could not get him for my heart to do it.

Grumio

Knock at the gate? O heavens! Spake you not these
40 words plain: 'Sirrah, knock me here; rap me here;
knock me well, and knock me soundly'? And come you
now with 'knocking at the gate'?

Petruchio

Sirrah, be gone, or talk not, I advise you.

Hortensio

Petruchio, patience, I am Grumio's pledge.
45 Why, this a heavy chance 'twixt him and you,
Your ancient, trusty, pleasant servant Grumio.
And tell me now, sweet friend, what happy gale
Blows you to Padua here, from old Verona?

Petruchio

Such wind as scatters young men through the world
50 To seek their fortunes farther than at home,
Where small experience grows. But in a few,
Signor Hortensio, thus it stands with me:
Antonio, my father, is deceased,
And I have thrust myself unto this maze,
55 Happily to wive and thrive as best I may.
Crowns in my purse I have, and goods at home,
And so am come abroad to see the world.

Hortensio

Petruchio, shall I then come roundly to thee
And wish thee to a shrewd ill-favoured wife?

56 *Crowns*: money.
57 *abroad*: away from home.
58 *come . . . thee*: tell you straight.
59 *wish thee to*: show you how to get.
   shrewd: shrewish.
   ill-favoured: bad tempered.
60 *Thou'dst . . . little*: you wouldn't thank
   me much.
63 *wish*: The sense is slightly different from
   that of 'wish' in line 59; Hortensio would
   not want his good friend to be married to
   a wife like Katherina.
67 *burden*: musical accompaniment.
68 *Florentius' love*: To save his life, Sir
   Florent (in Gower's *Confessio Amantis*,
   Book I) must find out what it is that
   women most desire. An old hag promises
   to tell him, on condition that he marries
   her. He accepts, and is told that all
   women want to be 'sovereign of man's
   love'. On the wedding-night the old
   woman, released from a magic spell when
   Lorent keeps his promise to marry her,
   turns back into a beautiful young girl. A
   version of the story is told by the Wife of
   Bath in Chaucer's *Canterbury Tales*.
69 *Sibyl*: A prophetess in classical mythology
   who asked the god Apollo to grant her as
   many years of life as the grains of sand
   that she held in her hand.
70 *Xanthippe*: The wife of Socrates, the
   Greek philosopher, was notorious for her
   bad temper.
71 *moves me not*: doesn't worry me.
72 *Affection's edge*: my keen desire.
74 *wive it wealthily*: make a rich marriage.
78 *aglet-baby*: Perhaps this was a little doll
   hanging (as a decorative tag) at the end of
   a lace.
   trot: hag.
79 *as . . . horses*: Horses, like cars, are
   always 'going wrong'; Grumio's
   comparison emphasizes the commercial
   aspect of Petruchio's wooing.
80 *so*: provided that.
82 *are . . . in*: have got so far in this matter.
83 *broached in jest*: started to suggest as a
   joke.

88 *intolerable curst*: unbearably bad-tempered.

89 *froward*: perverse.
   beyond all measure: extreme.
90 *state*: financial situation.

60 Thou'dst thank me but a little for my counsel;
   And yet I'll promise thee she shall be rich,
   And very rich. But thou'rt too much my friend,
   And I'll not wish thee to her.

   Petruchio
   Signor Hortensio, 'twixt such friends as we
65 Few words suffice; and therefore, if thou know
   One rich enough to be Petruchio's wife —
   As wealth is burden of my wooing dance —
   Be she as foul as was Florentius' love,
   As old as Sibyl, and as curst and shrewd
70 As Socrates' Xanthippe, or a worse,
   She moves me not — or not removes at least
   Affection's edge in me, were she as rough
   As are the swelling Adriatic seas.
   I come to wive it wealthily in Padua;
75 If wealthily, then happily in Padua.

   Grumio
   Nay, look you, sir, he tells you flatly what his mind is.
   Why, give him gold enough and marry him to a
   puppet or an aglet-baby, or an old trot with ne'er a
   tooth in her head, though she have as many diseases as
80 two and fifty horses. Why, nothing comes amiss, so
   money comes withal.

   Hortensio
   Petruchio, since we are stepped thus far in,
   I will continue that I broached in jest.
   I can, Petruchio, help thee to a wife
85 With wealth enough, and young and beauteous,
   Brought up as best becomes a gentlewoman.
   Her only fault, and that is faults enough,
   Is that she is intolerable curst,
   And shrewd, and froward, so beyond all measure
90 That, were my state far worser than it is,
   I would not wed her for a mine of gold.

Petruchio

Hortensio, peace: thou know'st not gold's effect;
Tell me her father's name and 'tis enough.
For I will board her though she chide as loud
95 As thunder when the clouds in autumn crack.

Hortensio

Her father is Baptista Minola,
An affable and courteous gentleman;
Her name is Katherina Minola,
Renowned in Padua for her scolding tongue.

Petruchio

100 I know her father, though I know not her,
And he knew my deceasèd father well.
I will not sleep, Hortensio, till I see her,
And therefore let me be thus bold with you,
To give you over at this first encounter,
105 Unless you will accompany me thither.

Grumio

[*To* Hortensio] I pray you sir, let him go while the
humour lasts. O' my word, an she knew him as well as
I do, she would think scolding would do little good
upon him. She may perhaps call him half a score
110 knaves or so: why, that's nothing; an he begin once,
he'll rail in his rope tricks. I'll tell you what, sir, an she
stand him but a little, he will throw a figure in her
face, and so disfigure her with it, that she shall have no
more eyes to see withal than a cat. You know him not,
sir.

Hortensio

115 Tarry, Petruchio, I must go with thee,
For in Baptista's keep my treasure is.
He hath the jewel of my life in hold,
His youngest daughter, beautiful Bianca,
And her withholds from me and other more,
120 Suitors to her and rivals in my love.
Supposing it a thing impossible,
For those defects I have before rehearsed,
That ever Katherina will be wooed.
Therefore this order hath Baptista ta'en,
125 That none shall have access unto Bianca
Till Katherine the curst have got a husband.

94 *board her*: woo her; Petruchio's image is from naval warfare.
   chide: grumble.

103 *thus bold*: so rude.
104 'To leave you now although we have only just met.'
105 *thither*: i.e. to Baptista's house.

106 *while . . . lasts*: as long as he is in this mood.

108 *do little good*: have no effect.
111 *in his rope-tricks*: in his own language; Grumio means 'rhetoric'.
   an: if.
112 *stand him*: argue with him.
112–3 *throw . . . with it*: answer her in such a way that will silence her. Grumio refers to a rhetorical figure of speech; when Kate is dis-figured, she will be bereft of language.

114 *eyes . . . cat*: Editors agree that these words do not make sense; perhaps the phrase should refer to a *blind* cat, suggesting that Petruchio has disfigured Kate by scratching her eyes out.
115 *Tarry*: wait a moment.
116 *keep*: keeping; a castle's 'keep' was the safe for all its treasures. Hortensio sustains a gentle word-play in the following lines.
117 *in hold*: in custody.
119 *withholds*: keeps.
   other: others. This use of the singular form is common in Elizabethan usage.
   more: as well as me.
121 *Supposing*: believing.
122 *before rehearsed*: just told you about.
124 *order . . . ta'en*: Baptista has made this plan.

126 *curst*: cursed; but the sense is not so strong as 'damned' — perhaps 'perverse', or 'wilful'.

129 *do me grace*: do me a favour.

130 *in sober robes*: wearing an academic gown.

132 *Well seen*: fully qualified.

134 *make love*: i.e. declare his love.

136 Grumio makes his comment directly to the audience, before drawing Hortensio's attention to the new arrivals.
beguile: deceive.

137 *lay . . . together*: make plots.

141 *a proper stripling*: a fine young man: Grumio is ironic.

142 *note*: i.e. the list of books.

143 *fairly bound*: Elizabethan books were often sold unbound, and the purchasers would put handsome covers on them.

144 *at any hand*: in any case.

145 *see . . . her*: make sure you don't teach her anything else.

147 *liberality*: generosity (in paying the tutor's wages).

148 *mend . . . largess*: add something as a present to you.
paper: i.e. the booklist referred to in line 142.

149 *them*: i.e. the books he has ordered; the Elizabethans liked to have things scented.

151 *read to her*: study with her.

154 *as . . . place*: as though you were present yourself.

Grumio
'Katherine the curst',
A title for a maid, of all titles the worst.
  Hortensio
Now shall my friend Petruchio do me grace,
130 And offer me disguised in sober robes
To old Baptista as a schoolmaster
Well seen in music, to instruct Bianca,
That so I may by this device at least
Have leave and leisure to make love to her,
135 And unsuspected court her by herself.

Enter Gremio *and* Lucentio (*disguised as* Cambio)

  Grumio
Here's no knavery! See, to beguile the old folks, how the young folks lay their heads together! — Master, master, look about you. Who goes there, ha?
  Hortensio
Peace, Grumio. It is the rival of my love.
140 Petruchio, stand by a while.
  Grumio
A proper stripling and an amorous!

Petruchio, Hortensio *and* Grumio
stand aside

  Gremio
[*To* Lucentio] O, very well, I have perused the note.
Hark you, sir, I'll have them very fairly bound,
All books of love; see that at any hand
145 And see you read no other lectures to her.
You understand me. Over and beside
Signor Baptista's liberality,
I'll mend it with a largess. Take your paper too.
And let me have them very well perfumed,
150 For she is sweeter than perfume itself
To whom they go to. What will you read to her?
  Lucentio
Whate'er I read to her, I'll plead for you
As for my patron, stand you so assured,
As firmly as yourself were still in place,
155 Yea, and perhaps with more successful words
Than you, unless you were a scholar, sir.

Gremio

O this learning, what a thing it is!

Grumio

[*Aside*] O this woodcock, what an ass it is!

Petruchio

[*Aside*] Peace, sirrah.

Hortensio

160 [*Aside*] Grumio, mum! — God save you, Signor
    Gremio.

Gremio

And you are well met, Signor Hortensio. Trow you
whither I am going? To Baptista Minola. I promised
to inquire carefully about a schoolmaster for the fair
Bianca, and by good fortune I have lighted well on this
165 young man, for learning and behaviour fit for her turn,
well read in poetry and other books — good ones, I
warrant ye.

Hortensio

'Tis well. And I have met a gentleman
Hath promised me to help me to another,
A fine musician to instruct our mistress.
170 So shall I no whit be behind in duty
To fair Bianca, so beloved of me.

Gremio

Beloved of me, and that my deeds shall prove.

Grumio

[*Aside*] And that his bags shall prove.

Hortensio

Gremio, 'tis now no time to vent our love.
175 Listen to me, and if you speak me fair,
I'll tell you news indifferent good for either.
Here is a gentleman whom by chance I met,
Upon agreement from us to his liking,
Will undertake to woo curst Katherine,
180 Yea, and to marry her, if her dowry please.

Gremio

So said, so done, is well.
Hortensio, have you told him all her faults?

Petruchio

I know she is an irksome brawling scold.
If that be all, masters, I hear no harm.

Gremio

185 No, say'st me so, friend? What countryman?

---

158 *woodcock*: a bird (of the snipe family) noted for its foolishness.

160 *mum*: keep quiet.

161 *Trow you*: do you know.

164 *lighted well*: discovered.
165 *fit . . . turn*: just what she needs.

173 *bags*: i.e. money-bags.

174 *vent*: talk about.
175 *speak me fair*: deal honestly with me.
176 *indifferent*: equally.
178 'If we can come to some agreement with him'; Hortensio wants to make Gremio share in the expenses of wooing Katherina.
181 *So . . . done*: Gremio's phrase seems to combine two proverbial sayings — 'No sooner said than done' *and* 'It is easier said than done'. He is happy to pay his share of Petruchio's expenses, but doubtful whether the scheme will work.
183 *irksome*: hateful (the sense is stronger than that of the modern usage).
     scold: quarrelsome woman.
185 *sayst me so*: is that all you have to say.
     What countryman: where are you from.

Petruchio
Born in Verona, old Antonio's son.
My father dead, my fortune lives for me,
And I do hope good days and long to see.
Gremio
O sir, such a life with such a wife were strange.
190 But if you have a stomach, to't a God's name;
You shall have me assisting you in all.
But will you woo this wildcat?
Petruchio
Will I live?
Grumio
Will he woo her? Ay, or I'll hang her.
Petruchio
195 Why came I hither but to that intent?
Think you a little din can daunt mine ears?
Have I not in my time heard lions roar?
Have I not heard the sea, puffed up with winds,
Rage like an angry boar chafed with sweat?
200 Have I not heard great ordnance in the field,
And heaven's artillery thunder in the skies?
Have I not in a pitched battle heard
Loud 'larums, neighing steeds, and trumpets' clang?
And do you tell me of a woman's tongue,
205 That gives not half so great a blow to hear
As will a chestnut in a farmer's fire?
Tush, tush, fear boys with bugs!
Grumio
                                        For he fears none.
Gremio
Hortensio, hark.
210 This gentleman is happily arrived,
My mind presumes, for his own good and yours.
Hortensio
I promised we would be contributors
And bear his charge of wooing, whatsoe'er.
Gremio
And so we will, provided that he win her.
Grumio
215 I would I were as sure of a good dinner.

Enter Tranio, brave *(disguised as*
Lucentio), *and* Biondello

---

188 *good . . . see*: to have a long and happy life.

190 *if . . . stomach*: if that's what you want.
     to't: get on with it.
     a: in

194 *or . . . her*: or be hanged to her. The sense of Grumio's comment is not immediately obvious, but it seems to be a dismissal of Katherina.
195 *to that intent*: for that purpose.
195–202 Petruchio's description of his heroic past fits him for a role as romantic lover — although it is probably fictitious.

199 *chafed*: enraged.
200 *ordnance*: cannon.
     field: battlefield.

203 *'larums*: battlecries.
     clang: the technical name for the sound of a military trumpet.

206 *chestnut*: i.e. the explosion of a roasted chestnut.
207 *fear . . . bugs*: frighten children with bugbears (= goblins).

210 *happily*: fortunately.
211 *yours*: Gremio tries to avoid paying Petruchio.

213 *charge of wooing*: the cost of his courtship.
     whatsoe'er: whatever it is.

215 *would*: wish.

215s.d. *brave*: finely dressed.

Tranio
Gentlemen, God save you. If I may be bold, tell me, I
beseech you, which is the readiest way to the house of
Signor Baptista Minola?

217 *readiest*: quickest.

Biondello
He that has the two fair daughters — is't he you
220 mean?

219 Biondello is playing a pre-arranged part.

Tranio
Even he, Biondello.

221 *Even he*: that's exactly the man I mean.

Gremio
Hark you, sir, you mean not her to—

222 *her to–*: Gremio suspects another rival,
come to woo Bianca; but Tranio is
impatient. The rhymed couplets of the
following lines suggest a battle of wits.

223 *What . . . do?*: what business is it of
yours?

224 *at any hand*: in any case.

Tranio
Perhaps him and her, sir. What have you to do?

Petruchio
Not her that chides, sir, at any hand, I pray.

Tranio
225 I love no chiders, sir. Biondello, let's away.

Lucentio
[*Aside to* Tranio] Well begun, Tranio.

Hortensio
Sir, a word ere you go.
Are you a suitor to the maid you talk of, yea or no?

Tranio
And if I be, sir, is it any offence?

Gremio
230 No, if without more words you will get you hence.

Tranio
Why, sir, I pray, are not the streets as free
For me as for you?

233 *so . . . she*: Bianca is not available for
Tranio to woo.

Gremio
                But so is not she.

Tranio
For what reason, I beseech you?

Gremio
235 For this reason, if you'll know,
That she's the choice love of Signor Gremio.

236 *choice*: chosen.

Hortensio
That she's the chosen of Signor Hortensio.

Tranio
Softly, my masters! If you be gentlemen,
Do me this right; hear me with patience.

238 *Softly*: take it easy; Tranio, pretending to
be Lucentio, tries to talk like a courtly
gentleman.

240 Baptista is a noble gentleman,
To whom my father is not all unknown,

244-7 Tranio is comparing Bianca to Helen
of Troy, the daughter of Leda and
Jupiter. She was said (in Greek
mythology) to be the most beautiful
woman in the world, and was stolen away
from her husband by Paris, son of Priam.
This was the cause of the Trojan War.

244-7 Tranio is comparing Bianca to Helen
of Troy, the daughter of Leda and
Jupiter. She was said (in Greek
mythology) to be the most beautiful
woman in the world, and was stolen away
from her husband by Paris, son of Priam.
This was the cause of the Trojan War.

247 *speed alone*: be the only one to succeed.

249 *give him head*: let him run on (as though
he were an unchecked horse).
a jade: a weak horse that will quickly tire.

And were his daughter fairer than she is,
She may more suitors have, and me for one.
Fair Leda's daughter had a thousand wooers,
245 Then well one more may fair Bianca have;
And so she shall: Lucentio shall make one,
Though Paris came, in hope to speed alone.

Gremio
What, this gentleman will out-talk us all!

Lucentio
Sir, give him head, I know he'll prove a jade.

Petruchio
250 Hortensio, to what end are all these words?

Hortensio
[*To* Tranio] Sir, let me be so bold as ask you,
Did you yet ever see Baptista's daughter?

Tranio
No, sir, but hear I do that he hath two:
The one as famous for a scolding tongue
255 As is the other for beauteous modesty.

256 *let her go by*: leave her alone.

257-8 Gremio considers the wooing of
Katherina to be a task equal to the twelve
apparently impossible labours imposed on
Hercules (whose family name was
Alcides).

259 *understand . . . sooth*: i.e. let me put it
plainly.

260 *hearken for*: are interested in.

Petruchio
Sir, sir, the first's for me, let her go by.

Gremio
Yea, leave that labour to great Hercules,
And let it be more than Alcides' twelve.

Petruchio
Sir, understand you this of me, in sooth:
260 The youngest daughter whom you hearken for
Her father keeps from all access of suitors
And will not promise her to any man
Until the elder sister first be wed.
The younger then is free, and not before.

Tranio
265 If it be so, sir, that you are the man

266 *stead*: help.

267 *break the ice*: get started.

269 *whose hap*: the man whose luck.

270 *graceless*: ill-bred.
ingrate: ungrateful.

271 *conceive*: understand.

273 *gratify*: reward; Hortensio is still
concerned that Petruchio shall be paid for
his task.

Must stead us all, and me amongst the rest,
And if you break the ice and do this feat,
Achieve the elder, set the younger free
For our access, whose hap shall be to have her
270 Will not so graceless be to be ingrate.

Hortensio
Sir, you say well, and well you do conceive;
And since you do profess to be a suitor,
You must, as we do, gratify this gentleman,
To whom we all rest generally beholding.

274 *generally*: together.
    beholding: indebted.
275 *slack*: slow in paying.
276 *contrive*: get together.
277 *quaff carouses . . . health*: do some
    drinking, toasting Bianca's health.
278 *as adversaries in law*: i.e. like the lawyers
    representing opposing sides.

280 *motion*: suggestion.

282 *I . . . venuto*: be my guest; the Italian
    words (which mean, literally, 'welcome')
    end the scene with a courtly flourish.

Tranio

275 Sir, I shall not be slack; in sign whereof,
Please ye we may contrive this afternoon,
And quaff carouses to our mistress' health,
And do as adversaries do in law,
Strive mightily, but eat and drink as friends.

Grumio *and* **Biondello**

280 O excellent motion! Fellows, let's be gone.

Hortensio

The motion's good indeed, and be it so.
Petruchio, I shall be your *ben venuto*.

[Exeunt

Act 2

Act 2 Scene 1

Baptista's two daughters are quarrelling, and
we are shown how Katherina has earned her
reputation. The suitors arrive, and Petruchio
announces his determination to woo Katherina.
Hortensio and Lucentio (calling themselves
Litio and Cambio) are presented as tutors;
Baptista sends them in to his daughters, whilst
he listens to Petruchio's marriage plans. Then,
with Gremio and Tranio (who is disguised as
Lucentio), Baptista leaves the stage, and at last
Katherina and Petruchio are brought together.
Their battle commences. On Baptista's return
he is told that the wedding will take place —
and he can now listen to the proposals of
Bianca's suitors. Gremio makes a generous
offer, but he is outbidden by Tranio.

3 *gawds*: trinkets — presumably jewellery
    given by her suitors.
4 *Unbind*: if you will unfasten.
5 *raiment*: clothes.
7 *my elders*: Such a reference to her age
    seems calculated to enrage Katherina.
8 *charge thee*: order you; 'thee' is omitted in
    the First Folio text.
13 *Minion*: A term of abuse for the spoilt
    favourite child.

14 *affect*: fancy, care for.
15 *but . . . him*: if there is no other way for
    you to have him.
16 *belike*: perhaps.
17 *fair*: fine, well-dressed.

18 *envy*: hate (the stress is on the second
    syllable).

Scene 1

Enter Katherina *and* Bianca (*with her
hands tied*)

Bianca
Good sister, wrong me not, nor wrong yourself,
To make a bondmaid and a slave of me.
That I disdain. But, for these other gawds,
Unbind my hands, I'll pull them off myself,
5 Yea, all my raiment, to my petticoat;
Or what you will command me will I do,
So well I know my duty to my elders.
Katherina
Of all thy suitors here I charge thee tell
Whom thou lov'st best; see thou dissemble not.
Bianca
10 Believe me, sister, of all the men alive
I never yet beheld that special face
Which I could fancy more than any other.
Katherina
Minion, thou liest. Is't not Hortensio?
Bianca
If you affect him, sister, here I swear
15 I'll plead for you myself but you shall have him.
Katherina
O, then belike you fancy riches more:
You will have Gremio to keep you fair.
Bianca
Is it for him you do envy me so?
Nay then you jest, and now I well perceive
20 You have but jested with me all this while.
I prithee, sister Kate, untie my hands.

Katherina
[*Striking her*] If that be jest, then all the rest
was so.

Enter Baptista

Baptista
Why, how now dame, whence grows this insolence?
—Bianca, stand aside. Poor girl, she weeps.
25 Go ply thy needle, meddle not with her.
[*To* Katherina] For shame, thou hilding of a
    devilish spirit,
Why dost thou wrong her that did ne'er wrong thee?
When did she cross thee with a bitter word?

Katherina
Her silence flouts me, and I'll be revenged.

She flies after Bianca

Baptista
30 What, in my sight! Bianca, get thee in.
                                           [*Exit* Bianca

Katherina
What, will you not suffer me? Nay, now I see
She is your treasure, she must have a husband,
I must dance barefoot on her wedding-day,
And for your love to her lead apes in hell.
35 Talk not to me, I will go sit and weep,
Till I can find occasion of revenge.   [*Exit

Baptista
Was ever gentleman thus grieved as I?
But who comes here?

Enter Gremio, Lucentio (*as* Cambio), *in
the habit of a mean man*; Petruchio, *with*
Hortensio (*as* Litio); *and* Tranio (*as*
Lucentio), *with his boy* Biondello, *bearing
a lute and books*

Gremio
Good morrow, neighbour Baptista.

Baptista
40 Good morrow, neighbour Gremio. God save you,
gentlemen.

Petruchio
And you, good sir. Pray have you not a daughter
Called Katherina, fair and virtuous?

23 *dame*: madam; a term of rebuke. Baptista's partiality for his younger daughter is evident, and partly explains Katherina's bitterness.
25 *ply thy needle*: get on with your sewing. *meddle not*: don't have anything to do.
26 *hilding*: baggage.
28 *cross*: annoy.
29 *flouts*: mocks.
31 *suffer me*: leave me alone.
33 *dance barefoot*: the proverbial fate of an elder sister when a younger married first.
34 *for*: because of. *lead apes in hell*: the proverbial fate of an unmarried woman, who could not lead children into heaven.
36 *occasion of*: opportunity for.
38s.d. *in the habit of a mean man*: dressed like an ordinary man (i.e. not like a gentleman).

Baptista
I have a daughter, sir, called Katherina.
Gremio

45 You are too blunt, go to it orderly.
Petruchio
You wrong me, Signor Gremio, give me leave.
I am a gentleman of Verona, sir,
That hearing of her beauty and her wit,
Her affability and bashful modesty,

50 Her wondrous qualities and mild behaviour,
Am bold to show myself a forward guest
Within your house, to make mine eye the witness
Of that report which I so oft have heard;
And for an entrance to my entertainment

55 I do present you with a man of mine,
[*Presents* Hortensio]
Cunning in music and the mathematics,
To instruct her fully in those sciences,
Whereof I know she is not ignorant.
Accept of him, or else you do me wrong.

60 His name is Litio, born in Mantua.
Baptista
You're welcome, sir, and he for your good sake.
But for my daughter Katherine, this I know,
She is not for your turn, the more my grief.
Petruchio
I see you do not mean to part with her,

65 Or else you like not of my company.
Baptista
Mistake me not, I speak but as I find.
Whence are you, sir? What may I call your name?
Petruchio
Petruchio is my name, Antonio's son,
A man well known throughout all Italy.
Baptista

70 I know him well. You are welcome for his sake.
Gremio
Saving your tale, Petruchio, I pray let us that are poor
petitioners speak too. Baccare! You are marvellous
forward.
Petruchio
O pardon me, Signor Gremio, I would fain be
doing.

45 *go . . . orderly*: talk properly.

51 *forward*: eager.

54 *for an entrance*: as an entrance-fee.
entertainment: hospitable reception.

56 *Cunning*: expert.
57 *sciences*: subjects.

61 *he*: i.e. he is welcome.

63 *for your turn*: the girl you want.

67 *What . . . name*: Baptista questions with
old-fashioned courtesy.

71 *Saving your tale*: With all respect to you.
72 *poor petitioners*: humble suitors.
Baccare: stand back.

74 *I . . . doing*: I want to get on with it.

Gremio

75 I doubt it not, sir, but you will curse your wooing.
—Neighbour, this is a gift very grateful, I am sure of it.
[*To* Baptista] To express the like kindness, myself, that
have been more kindly beholding to you than any,
freely give unto you this young scholar [*Presents*
80 Lucentio] that hath been long studying at Rheims, as
cunning in Greek, Latin, and other languages as the
other in music and mathematics. His name is Cambio;
pray accept his service.

Baptista

A thousand thanks, Signor Gremio. Welcome, good
85 Cambio. [*To* Tranio] But, gentle sir, methinks you
walk like a stranger. May I be so bold to know the
cause of your coming?

Tranio

Pardon me, sir, the boldness is mine own
That, being a stranger in this city here,
90 Do make myself a suitor to your daughter,
Unto Bianca, fair and virtuous;
Nor is your firm resolve unknown to me
In the preferment of the eldest sister.
This liberty is all that I request,
95 That, upon knowledge of my parentage,
I may have welcome 'mongst the rest that woo,
And free access and favour as the rest.
And toward the education of your daughters
I here bestow a simple instrument,
100 And this small packet of Greek and Latin books.
If you accept them, then their worth is great.

Baptista

Lucentio is your name? Of whence, I pray?

Tranio

Of Pisa, sir, son to Vincentio.

Baptista

A mighty man of Pisa; by report,
105 I know him well. You are very welcome, sir.
[*To* Hortensio] Take you the lute, [*To* Lucentio]
    and you the set of books,
You shall go see your pupils presently.
Holla, within!

76 *a gift*: i.e. the presentation of Hortensio.
77 *like*: same.
78 *kindly*: naturally; Gremio implies that Baptista has favoured him as a suitor to Bianca.
80 *Rheims*: a famous university in northern France.
    cunning in: knowledgeable about.
81 *the other*: i.e. Hortensio.
82 *Cambio*: The name that Lucentio has adopted means 'exchange' in Italian.

92 *resolve*: resolution.
93 *preferment*: i.e. the insistence that Katherina must be married before Bianca.
99 *instrument*: i.e. the lute that Biondello is carrying.

102 *Lucentio . . . name*: Perhaps Baptista reads Lucentio's name in one of the books.
104 *by report*: from what I hear.
107 *presently*: immediately.

Enter a Servant

Sirrah, lead these gentlemen

110 To my daughters, and tell them both
These are their tutors. Bid them use them well.
    [*Exeunt* Servant, Hortensio, Lucentio *and* Biondello
We will go walk a little in the orchard,
And then to dinner. You are passing welcome,
And so I pray you all to think yourselves.

Petruchio

115 Signor Baptista, my business asketh haste,
And every day I cannot come to woo.
You knew my father well, and in him me,
Left solely heir to all his lands and goods,
Which I have bettered rather than decreased.

120 Then tell me, if I get your daughter's love,
What dowry shall I have with her to wife?

Baptista

After my death the one half of my lands,
And in possession twenty thousand crowns.

Petruchio

And for that dowry I'll assure her of

125 Her widowhood, be it that she survive me,
In all my lands and leases whatsoever.
Let specialties be therefore drawn between us,
That covenants may be kept on either hand.

Baptista

Ay, when the special thing is well obtained,

130 That is, her love; for that is all in all.

Petruchio

Why, that is nothing; for I tell you, father,
I am as peremptory as she proud-minded,
And where two raging fires meet together
They do consume the thing that feeds their fury.

135 Though little fire grows great with little wind
Yet extreme gusts will blow out fire and all.
So I to her, and so she yields to me,
For I am rough and woo not like a babe.

Baptista

Well mayst thou woo, and happy be thy speed!

140 But be thou armed for some unhappy words.

---

113 *passing*: exceedingly.

115 *asketh*: demands.
116 *every . . . woo*: This line is found in
several old English ballads.
117 *in him me*: because of him you know me.
118 *solely heir*: the only heir.

121 *dowry*: the father's financial settlement on
his daughter.

123 *in possession*: at the time of marriage; this
cash settlement may have been unusually
high because of Katherina's temper.
124 *for*: in return for.
125 *Her widowhood*: a widow's rights (the
exact terms would be specified in the
marriage contract; without these, the
estate would pass to the next male heir).
126 *lands . . . whatsoever*: his estate; Petruchio
uses the correct legal terminology.
127 *specialties*: precise contracts.
128 *covenants*: formal agreements.
on either hand: between both parties.
131 *father*: Petruchio's familiarity shows his
self-confidence.
132 *peremptory*: masterful; the stress is on the
first syllable.

137 *So I to her*: Petruchio will be like a strong
wind to Katherina, who has hitherto met
only light winds that have fanned, not
extinguished, the fire of her temperament.
139 *happy be thy speed*: good luck to you.

141 *to the proof*: with armour that is impenetrable.
142 *shakes*: The 's' ending for third-person plural is common in Shakespeare.
142s.d. *broke*: bleeding. This episode with Hortensio demonstrates both Katherina's violence, and Petruchio's resolution.

144 *promise*: assure.

145 *prove . . . musician*: become a good musician.

146 *prove a soldier*: put a soldier to the test; Hortensio plays with the two meanings of 'prove'.
147 *hold with*: resist.
148 *break*: train (as a horse is broken).

149 *broke the lute*: In some modern productions of this play, Hortensio enters with the lute broken over his head.
150 *frets*: ridges on the lute to position the fingers.
153 *Frets*: irritations.

157 *pillory*: device for imprisoning a wrong-doer by restraining head and arms.

160 *As had she*: as though she had. *misuse*: abuse.

161 *lusty*: spirited.

165 *Proceed in practice*: continue your teaching.
166 *apt*: ready.

Petruchio
Ay, to the proof, as mountains are for winds
That shakes not though they blow perpetually.

Enter Hortensio (*as* Litio)
with his head broke

Baptista
How now, my friend, why dost thou look so pale?
Hortensio
For fear, I promise you, if I look pale.
Baptista
145 What, will my daughter prove a good musician?
Hortensio
I think she'll sooner prove a soldier.
Iron may hold with her, but never lutes.
Baptista
Why then thou canst not break her to the lute?
Hortensio
Why no, for she hath broke the lute to me.
150 I did but tell her she mistook her frets,
And bowed her hand to teach her fingering,
When, with a most impatient devilish spirit,
'Frets, call you these?' quoth she, 'I'll fume with them'
And with that word she struck me on the head,
155 And through the instrument my pate made way,
And there I stood amazèd for a while,
As on a pillory, looking through the lute,
While she did call me 'rascal', 'fiddler',
And 'twangling Jack', with twenty such vile terms,
160 As had she studied to misuse me so.
Petruchio
Now, by the world, it is a lusty wench;
I love her ten times more than e'er I did.
O how I long to have some chat with her!
Baptista
[*To* Hortensio] Well, go with me, and be not so discomfited.
165 Proceed in practice with my younger daughter;
She's apt to learn and thankful for good turns.
—Signor Petruchio, will you go with us
Or shall I send my daughter Kate to you?

Petruchio

I pray you do. I'll attend her here—
                    [*Exeunt all but* Petruchio

170 And woo her with some spirit when she comes.
Say that she rail, why then I'll tell her plain
She sings as sweetly as a nightingale.
Say that she frown, I'll say she looks as clear
As morning roses newly washed with dew.
175 Say she be mute and will not speak a word,
Then I'll commend her volubility
And say she uttereth piercing eloquence.
If she do bid me pack, I'll give her thanks,
As though she bid me stay by her a week.
180 If she deny to wed, I'll crave the day
When I shall ask the banns, and when be marrièd.
But here she comes, and now, Petruchio, speak.

Enter Katherina

Good morrow, Kate — for that's your name, I hear.
Katherina
Well have you heard, but something hard of
    hearing:
185 They call me Katherine that do talk of me.
Petruchio
You lie, in faith, for you are called plain Kate,
And bonny Kate, and sometimes Kate the curst.
But Kate, the prettiest Kate in Christendom,
Kate of Kate Hall, my super-dainty Kate,
190 For dainties are all Kates, and therefore, Kate,
Take this of me, Kate of my consolation:
Hearing thy mildness praised in every town,
Thy virtues spoke of, and thy beauty sounded,
Yet not so deeply as to thee belongs,
195 Myself am moved to woo thee for my wife.
Katherina
'Moved', in good time! Let him that moved you
    hither
Remove you hence. I knew you at the first
You were a movable.
Petruchio
Why, what's a movable?
Katherina
200 A joined stool.

---

170 *attend*: wait for.

171 *rail*: shout at me.

177 *piercing*: moving.
178 *pack*: go away, clear off.

180 *deny*: refuse.
      crave the day: ask her to name the day.
181 *ask the banns*: In the Church of England,
      a marriage must be publicly declared on
      three successive Sundays before the
      ceremony can take place; this is not, in
      fact, done in the play.
184 *heard . . . hard*: The pronunciation of
      these words would be the same, allowing
      Katherina to make a pun. The following
      exchange of witty insults, usually
      involving a play on words, must be acted
      very fast.

188 *Christendom*: the entire Christian world.
189 *Kate Hall*: This may have been some kind
      of topical joke, whose sense is now lost.
190 *dainties are all Kates*: delicacies are all
      called cates.
191 *consolation*: comfort.
193 *sounded*: proclaimed; but the word also
      means 'fathomed' — hence the next line's
      pun.
194 *to thee belongs*: as you deserve.

196 *in good time*: indeed.

198 *a movable*: a piece of furniture that can be
      moved.

200 *A joined stool*: stool made by a joiner (a
      common insult).

201 *hit it*: got it right.
202 *bear*: Petruchio picks up Kate's use of
     'bear' (= to carry burdens) and adds two
     further senses — to bear children, *and* to
     bear the weight of a lover.
204 *No . . . you*: i.e. you would not have the
     (sexual) stamina for me.
206 *light*: light in weight, *and* frivolous,
     wanton.
207 'Too quick-witted to be caught by a
     country fellow like you.'
208 *as heavy*: Katherina uses the imagery of
     coinage in order to indulge this
     light/heavy antithesis; her meaning is that
     she is one hundred percent honest —
     counterfeit coins, made of base metal,
     weighed less than genuine ones.
209 *buzz*: The sound made by a bee (so
     allowing Petruchio a rather feeble pun);
     also a noise of contempt, as Petruchio
     dismisses Katherina's account of herself.
     ta'en: caught.
     a buzzard: A kind of hawk which is
     unteachable and which takes the wrong
     prey.
211 *turtle*: turtle-dove, symbol of faithful love.
212 *buzzard*: buzzing insect (e.g. a wasp);
     Katherina seems to be saying that the
     buzzard who catches a dove is making a
     mistake like that of the dove who catches
     the wasp.
217-22 Shakespeare is setting up a favourite
     old joke, punning on the sound of 'tail'
     and 'tale', and leading up to an obscene
     use of 'tail', which gives Petruchio the
     victory in this first verbal battle.

Petruchio
Thou hast hit it. Come, sit on me.
    Katherina
Asses are made to bear, and so are you.
    Petruchio
Women are made to bear, and so are you.
    Katherina
No such jade as you, if me you mean.
    Petruchio
205 Alas, good Kate, I will not burden thee,
For knowing thee to be but young and light—
    Katherina
Too light for such a swain as you to catch,
And yet as heavy as my weight should be.
    Petruchio
'Should be'? Should — buzz!
    Katherina   Well ta'en, and like a
210 buzzard.
    Petruchio
O slow-winged turtle, shall a buzzard take thee?
    Katherina
Ay, for a turtle, as he takes a buzzard.
    Petruchio
Come, come, you wasp, i'faith you are too angry.
    Katherina
If I be waspish, best beware my sting.
    Petruchio
215 My remedy is then to pluck it out.

222 *come again*: have another try; Petruchio is
    preparing to start a fresh battle of words.
224 *try*: put to the test.
225 *cuff*: hit.
226 *So*: in that way.
    arms: coat of arms, which indicated the
    status of a gentleman.

229 *put me in thy books*: To be entered in the
    herald's books was the sign of a
    gentleman; and to be in a person's (good)
    books was to be in favour.
230 *crest*: device borne above the shield and
    helmet in a coat of arms; *and* the feathers
    on a bird's head.
    coxcomb: fool's cap (in the shape of a
    cock's comb).

231 *combless*: harmless (the comb was cut off,
    or failed to grow, on a castrated — and
    therefore unaggressive — male bird).
    so: provided that.
232 *craven*: a cock that gives up easily, and
    admits defeat by dropping its crest;
    Katherina has won this round of the
    fight.

234 *crab*: crab-apple — a wild apple that is
    very sour.

Katherina
Ay, if the fool could find it where it lies.
   Petruchio
Who knows not where a wasp does wear his sting?
In his tail.
      Katherina
        In his tongue
      Petruchio
220   Whose tongue?
      Katherina
Yours if you talk of tales, and so farewell.
      Petruchio
What, with my tongue in your tail? Nay, come
  again.
Good Kate, I am a gentleman—
       Katherina
That I'll try.

       She strikes him

      Petruchio
225 I swear I'll cuff you if you strike again.
      Katherina
So may you lose your arms.
If you strike me, you are no gentleman,
And if no gentleman, why then no arms.
      Petruchio
A herald, Kate? O put me in thy books!
      Katherina
230 What is your crest — a coxcomb?
      Petruchio
A combless cock, so Kate will be my hen.
      Katherina
No cock of mine, you crow too like a craven.
      Petruchio
Nay, come, Kate, come, you must not look so sour.
      Katherina
It is my fashion when I see a crab.
      Petruchio
235 Why, here's no crab, and therefore look not sour.
      Katherina
There is, there is.
      Petruchio
Then show it me.

237 *glass*: looking-glass.

Katherina   Had I a glass, I would.
Petruchio
What, you mean my face?
Katherina
Well aimed of such a young one.
Petruchio

239 *Well aimed*: a good guess.
of: for.

240 *too young*: too strong.

240 Now, by Saint George, I am too young for you.
Katherina
Yet you are withered.
Petruchio   'Tis with cares.
Katherina   I care not.
Petruchio
Nay, hear you, Kate. In sooth, you scape not so.
Katherina

243 *I chafe you*: it will only excite you.

I chafe you if I tarry. Let me go.
Petruchio

244 *not a whit*: not at all.
passing: exceedingly.
245 *coy*: disdainful.
246 *report . . . liar*: what they say is all lies.
247 *gamesome*: full of fun.
courteous: lady-like.

249 *look askance*: glare.

No, not a whit; I find you passing gentle.
245 'Twas told me you were rough, and coy, and sullen,
And now I find report a very liar,
For thou art pleasant, gamesome, passing courteous,
But slow in speech, yet sweet as spring-time flowers;
Thou canst not frown, thou canst not look askance,

251 *cross*: perverse.

253 *conference*: conversation.

250 Nor bite the lip, as angry wenches will,
Nor hast thou pleasure to be cross in talk;
But thou with mildness entertain'st thy wooers,
With gentle conference, soft and affable.
Why does the world report that Kate doth limp?
255 O slanderous world! Kate like the hazel-twig
Is straight and slender, and as brown in hue
As hazel-nuts and sweeter than the kernels.
O let me see thee walk: thou dost not halt.
Katherina

258 *halt*: limp.

259 *whom . . . command*: A proverbial saying
— 'give orders to your servants'.

260 *Dian . . . grove*: Diana, classical goddess
of chastity, was traditionally worshipped
in a grove.
become: adorn.
261 *gait*: movements, walking.
263 *sportful*: playful.

264 *study*: learn.

265 *It is extempore*: I just made it up.
mother-wit: natural genius.

Go, fool, and whom thou keep'st command.
Petruchio
260 Did ever Dian so become a grove
As Kate this chamber with her princely gait?
O be thou Dian, and let her be Kate,
And then let Kate be chaste and Dian sportful.
Katherina
Where did you study all this goodly speech?
Petruchio
265 It is extempore, from my mother-wit.

266 *else*: otherwise.

Katherina
A witty mother, witless else her son.
Petruchio
Am I not wise?
Katherina
                          Yes, keep you warm.

268 *keep you warm*: i.e. with just enough sense
to keep you warm (a proverbial saying).

269 *Marry*: by (the Virgin) Mary.
mean: intend to.

271 *in plain terms*: to speak plainly.

272 *'greed*: agreed.

273 *will you, nill you*: whether you like it or
not (a proverbial phrase that survives as
'willy, nilly').

274 *for your turn*: just right for you.

Petruchio
Marry, so I mean, sweet Katherine, in thy bed.
270 And therefore, setting all this chat aside,
Thus in plain terms: your father hath consented
That you shall be my wife; your dowry 'greed on;
And will you, nill you, I will marry you.
Now, Kate, I am a husband for your turn,
275 For by this light whereby I see thy beauty,
Thy beauty that doth make me like thee well.
Thou must be married to no man but me.
For I am he am born to tame you, Kate,
And bring you from a wild Kate to a Kate

279 *wild Kate*: Perhaps there is a pun with
'wildcat'.
280 *Conformable*: tame, submissive.

280 Conformable as other household Kates.
Here comes your father.

                Enter Baptista, Gremio *and* Tranio (*as*
                Lucentio)

                          Never make denial;
I must and will have Katherine to my wife.

281 *Never make denial*: don't refuse me.
282 *to*: for.

283 *how speed you*: how are you getting on.

Baptista
Now, Signor Petruchio, how speed you with my
daughter?
Petruchio
How but well sir? How but well?
285 It were impossible I should speed amiss.

285 *speed amiss*: get on badly.

Baptista
Why, how now, daughter Katherine? In your
dumps?

286 *In your dumps*: The modern form is
'down in the dumps' — i.e. miserable.

Katherina
Call you me 'daughter'? Now I promise you
You have showed a tender fatherly regard,
To wish me wed to one half-lunatic,
290 A madcap ruffian and a swearing Jack,
That thinks with oaths to face the matter out.

290 *Jack*: knave, rascal.
291 *face*: brazen.

Petruchio
Father, 'tis thus: yourself and all the world
That talked of her, have talked amiss of her.

292 *all the world*: everybody.
293 *talked amiss of*: been wrong about.

294 *curst*: bad-tempered.
for policy: deliberately, with some purpose.
295 *froward*: wilfully perverse.
296 *hot*: hot-tempered.
297 *Grissel*: Griselda was the model of wifely patience and long-suffering. Her story was first told in Boccaccio's *Decameron*, and later by Chaucer in *The Clerk's Tale*.
298 *Lucrece*: In his narrative poem *The Rape of Lucrece*, Shakespeare told the famous story of the Roman matron who killed herself after she had been raped by Tarquin.
303 *speeding*: success.
goodnight our part: we can say goodbye to our share in the business (i.e. both to their promises to pay Petruchio's expenses and to their hopes of gaining Bianca).

306 *'twixt us twain*: between the two of us.
being alone: when we were alone.
307 *still*: always.

311 *vied*: redoubled: in gambling, this is a term used for raising the stakes.
protesting: swearing.
312 *in a twink*: i.e. 'in the twinkling of an eye'.
313 *'Tis a world*: it is worth a world.
315 *meacock*: feeble.
316 *will*: will go.
317 *'gainst*: ready for.
318 *bid*: invite.

321 *'tis a match*: Baptista pronounces what, for the purposes of the play, must be considered as a formal marriage contract — something more than an engagement but less than a wedding.

324 *apace*: quickly.

326 *we . . . Sunday*: Petruchio might sing these words, which form the refrain in several old ballads.

327 *clapped up*: fixed up.

If she be curst, it is for policy,
295 For she's not froward, but modest as the dove;
She is not hot, but temperate as the morn;
For patience she will prove a second Grissel,
And Roman Lucrece for her chastity;
And to conclude, we have 'greed so well together
300 That upon Sunday is the wedding-day.

Katherina
I'll see thee hanged on Sunday first.

Gremio
Hark, Petruchio, she says she'll see thee hanged first.

Tranio
Is this your speeding? Nay then, good-night our part.

Petruchio
Be patient, gentlemen, I choose her for myself;
305 If she and I be pleased, what's that to you?
'Tis bargained 'twixt us twain, being alone,
That she shall still be curst in company.
I tell you 'tis incredible to believe
How much she loves me. O, the kindest Kate,
310 She hung about my neck, and kiss on kiss
She vied so fast, protesting oath on oath,
That in a twink she won me to her love.
O, you are novices! 'Tis a world to see
How tame, when men and women are alone,
315 A meacock wretch can make the curstest shrew.
Give me thy hand, Kate, I will unto Venice,
To buy apparel 'gainst the wedding-day.
Provide the feast, father, and bid the guests.
I will be sure my Katherine shall be fine.

Baptista
320 I know not what to say, but give me your hands.
God send you joy; Petruchio, 'tis a match.

Gremio *and* Tranio
Amen, say we. We will be witnesses.

Petruchio
Father, and wife, and gentlemen, adieu,
I will to Venice, Sunday comes apace.
325 We will have rings, and things, and fine array,
And kiss me, Kate, we will be married o'Sunday.
[*Exeunt* Petruchio *and* Katherina *separately*

Gremio
Was ever match clapped up so suddenly?

328 *I play . . . part*: I'm acting like a trader.
329 *a desperate mart*: a risky market.
330 *commodity*: piece of merchandise.
   lay fretting by you: was going to waste;
   and was irritating you.
331 *gain*: profit.
   perish on the seas: i.e. as exports can be
   lost at sea.
334 *looked for*: been waiting for.
339 *Youngling*: young man.
   dear: affectionately; *and* with as much
   expense.
340 *fry*: is too hot; the word, however, was
   chosen for the rhyme.
341 *Skipper*: playboy, irresponsible youth.
   nourisheth: can provide.
343 *compound*: settle.
344 *deeds*: actions; *and* legal documents —
   marriage settlements.
   he of both: whichever of you two;
   Hortensio has been forgotten.
345 *dower*: that part of his estate which a
   husband leaves (in his will) to his wife —
   cf. Petruchio's provision for Katherina's
   'widowhood' in lines 122–4.
349 *plate*: domestic utensils of silver and gold.
350 *lave*: wash.
351 *hangings . . . tapestry*: The best quality
   wall-coverings; Tyre, a famous trading-
   centre, was also famous from classical
   times for the manufacture of a rich purple
   dye.

352 *coffers*: money-chests.
353 *cypress*: wood prized for its fragrance.
   arras counterpoints: bedcovers
   (counterpanes) from Arras in Flanders
   (also famous for its tapestries).
354 *tents*: testers — bed-curtains.
   canopies: i.e. for the beds.

Baptista
Faith, gentlemen, now I play a merchant's part,
And venture madly on a desperate mart.
    Tranio
330 'Twas a commodity lay fretting by you;
'Twill bring you gain, or perish on the seas.
    Baptista
The gain I seek is quiet in the match.
    Gremio
No doubt but he hath got a quiet catch.
But now, Baptista, to your younger daughter:
335 Now is the day we long have looked for;
I am your neighbour, and was suitor first.
    Tranio
And I am one that love Bianca more
Than words can witness or your thoughts can guess.
    Gremio
Youngling, thou canst not love so dear as I.
    Tranio
340 Greybeard, thy love doth freeze.
    Gremio   But thine doth fry.
Skipper, stand back, 'tis age that nourisheth.
    Tranio
But youth in ladies' eyes that flourisheth.
    Baptista
Content you, gentlemen, I will compound this strife.
'Tis deeds must win the prize, and he of both
345 That can assure my daughter greatest dower
Shall have my Bianca's love.
Say, Signor Gremio, what can you assure her?
    Gremio
First, as you know, my house within the city
Is richly furnishèd with plate and gold,
350 Basins and ewers to lave her dainty hands;
My hangings all of Tyrian tapestry;
In ivory coffers I have stuffed my crowns,
In cypress chests my arras counterpoints,
Costly apparel, tents and canopies,
355 Fine linen, Turkey cushions bossed with pearl,
Valance of Venice gold in needlework,
Pewter and brass, and all things that belongs
To house or housekeeping; then at my farm
I have a hundred milch-kine to the pail,

355 *Turkey*: English trade with Turkey was developing at the time of this play, and the imports were expensive; Gremio is trying to impress Baptista.
bossed: embossed, richly embroidered.

356 *Valance*: drapery hanging from the bed canopies.
Venice . . . needlework: embroidered with gold thread from Venice.

357 *things that belongs*: It is not uncommon for Shakespeare to use a singular verb form with the relative pronoun — 'that' — when the antecedent — 'things' — is plural.

359 *milch-kine*: cows giving milk.
to the pail: for the dairy (not for feeding calves).

360 *oxen*: beef cattle.

361 *answerable . . . portion*: in proportion to this estate.

362 *struck in years*: handicapped by age.

365 *came well in*: was well said.
list: listen.

368 *three or four*: Tranio (pretending to be Lucentio) increases the bidding.

369 *Pisa walls*: the walls of Pisa.

371–2 *two thousand . . . fruitful land*: a large annual income from fertile land.

372 *jointure*: estate settled on a woman at the time of her marriage — compare 'widow-hood' (line 122) and 'dower' (line 345).

373 *pinched you*: got you there.

376 *argosy*: largest class of merchant vessel.

377 *Marseilles' road*: the sheltered water outside the harbour of Marseilles; the spelling of the Folio text indicates the pronunciation — 'Marcellus'.

378 *choked*: i.e. beaten your offer.

380 *galliasses*: ships, larger than galleys, using both sails and oars.

381 *tight*: sound-watertight.

387 *out-vied*: outbidden; see line 311.

390 *else*: otherwise.

392 *cavil*: legal trifle.

360 Six-score fat oxen standing in my stalls,
And all things answerable to this portion.
Myself am struck in years, I must confess,
And if I die tomorrow this is hers,
If whilst I live she will be only mine.

Tranio
365 That 'only' came well in. Sir, list to me.
I am my father's heir and only son;
If I may have your daughter to my wife,
I'll leave her houses three or four as good
Within rich Pisa walls as any one
370 Old Signor Gremio has in Padua,
Besides two thousand ducats by the year
Of fruitful land, all which shall be her jointure.
What, have I pinched you, Signor Gremio?

Gremio
Two thousand ducats by the year of land?
375 [*Aside*] My land amounts not to so much in all.
—That she shall have, besides an argosy
That now is lying in Marseilles' road.
[*To* Tranio] What, have I choked you with an argosy?

Tranio
Gremio, 'tis known my father hath no less
380 Than three great argosies, besides two galliasses
And twelve tight galleys. These I will assure her,
And twice as much whate'er thou offer'st next.

Gremio
Nay, I have offered all, I have no more,
And she can have no more than all I have.
385 [*To* Baptista] If you like me, she shall have me and mine.

Tranio
Why then the maid is mine from all the world
By your firm promise; Gremio is out-vied.

Baptista
I must confess your offer is the best,
And let your father make her the assurance,
390 She is your own; else, you must pardon me.
If you should die before him, where's her dower?

Tranio
That's but a cavil; he is old, I young.

393 Gremio resorts to a platitude, proverbially
    phrased as 'Young men may die, old men
    must die'.

Gremio
And may not young men die as well as old?
Baptista
Well gentlemen,
395 I am thus resolved: on Sunday next you know
My daughter Katherine is to be married;
Now, on the Sunday following shall Bianca
Be bride [*To* Tranio] to you, if you make this
    assurance;
If not, to Signor Gremio.
400 And so I take my leave, and thank you both.

                                        [*Exit*

Gremio
Adieu, good neighbour. —Now I fear thee not;
Sirrah, young gamester, your father were a fool

402 *gamester*: gambler.
    were: would be.
403 *waning age*: 'declining years'.
404 *Set . . . table*: be dependent on you.
    toy: ridiculous idea.
405 *not so kind*: i.e. cannot be fooled so easily.
406 *A vengeance on*: damn you.
407 *faced . . . ten*: The expression, deriving
    from a card-game called Primero, seems to
    indicate that Tranio is winning at the
    moment — by bluffing.
409 *see no reason*: can't see any other way.
    supposed Lucentio: the man who is
    supposed to be Lucentio — i.e. himself.
410 *supposed Vincentio*: who is supposed to be
    Vincentio (Lucentio's father — see *1, 2,*
    13).
412 *get*: beget.

To give thee all, and in his waning age
Set foot under thy table. Tut, a toy,
405 An old Italian fox is not so kind, my boy!

                                        [*Exit*

Tranio
A vengeance on your crafty withered hide!
Yet I have faced it with a card of ten.
'Tis in my head to do my master good.
I see no reason but supposed Lucentio
410 Must get a father, called supposed Vincentio,
And that's a wonder: fathers commonly
Do get their children, but in this case of wooing
A child shall get a sire, if I fail not of my cunning.

                                        [*Exit*

Act 3

Act 3 Scene 1

Lucentio and Hortensio are competing for Bianca's love whilst they give her lessons in Latin and music. Bianca responds well to Lucentio, but rejects the tutor whom she knows as Litio (the disguised Hortensio). She leaves them both to help with the preparations for her sister's wedding-day.

1 *forward*: impertinent; perhaps Hortensio was guiding Bianca's hand in the same way that he had tried to teach Katherina (2, 1, 149).
2 *entertainment*: reception.
4 *wrangling*: The term used for academic debates in the universities.
5 *The patroness*: In the Christian church, St Cecilia is the patron saint of music; Hortensio is flattering Bianca.
6 *prerogative*: precedence; music was held to be the highest form of study.
8 *lecture*: lesson.
leisure for as much: just as much time; Hortensio speaks pompously.
9 *Preposterous*: i.e. 'You've got things the wrong way round'; Lucentio shows a pedantic turn of phrase in his literal use of this adjective — which, used more loosely, means 'ridiculous'.
read: studied.
10 *ordained*: instituted by God.
12 *usual pain*: normal work.
13 *read*: give a lesson in.
14 *serve in*: serve up; Lucentio is dismissive of his rival's music.
15 *braves*: insults.
16 *do me double wrong*: both wrong me.
17 *resteth in my choice*: is for me to decide.
18 'You can't treat me like a schoolboy.'

Scene 1

Enter Lucentio (*as* Cambio), Hortensio (*as* Litio), *and* Bianca

Lucentio
Fiddler, forbear, you grow too forward, sir.
Have you so soon forgot the entertainment
Her sister Katherine welcomed you withal?
Hortensio
But, wrangling pedant, this is
5 The patroness of heavenly harmony!
Then give me leave to have prerogative;
And when in music we have spent an hour,
Your lecture shall have leisure for as much.
Lucentio
Preposterous ass, that never read so far
10 To know the cause why music was ordained!
Was it not to refresh the mind of man
After his studies or his usual pain?
Then give me leave to read philosophy
And while I pause serve in your harmony.
Hortensio
15 Sirrah, I will not bear these braves of thine.
Bianca
Why, gentlemen, you do me double wrong
To strive for that which resteth in my choice.
I am no breeching scholar in the schools,
I'll not be tied to hours nor 'pointed times,
20 But learn my lessons as I please myself.
And, to cut off all strife, here sit we down,
Take you your instrument, play you the whiles;
His lecture will be done ere you have tuned.

19 *'pointed*: appointed.
21 *to cut off all strife*: to stop the argument.
22 *the whiles*: for a time.
24 *I am in tune*: i.e. when my lute is in tune; but Lucentio takes the remark literally.

26 *left we last*: did we stop reading.

28-9 Lucentio reads two lines from Ovid's *Heroides* (i.33-4): 'Here ran the river Simois, here is the Sigeian land. Here stood old Priam's lofty palace.'
30 *Conster*: translate; Bianca uses an old form (stressed on the first syllable) of 'construe'.
31 *as . . . before*: Lucentio's mock translation gives him a chance to declare his love.

35 *bearing my port*: taking my place.
36 *beguile*: cheat.
    pantaloon: i.e. Gremio; compare *1, 1, 47*s.d. Lucentio does not think of the disguised Hortensio as a rival.
38 *jars*: is discordant.

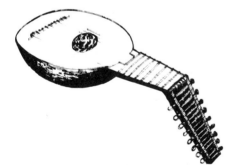

39 *Spit in the hole*: This might have made the lute-pegs tighter, keeping the tension on the strings; Lucentio adapts a proverbial saying to encourage a second attempt: 'Spit in your hands and take better hold'.
40-43 Bianca repeats the Latin of her lesson, but offers her own words to warn and counsel her teacher/lover.

Hortensio
You'll leave his lecture when I am in tune?
Lucentio
25 That will be never. Tune your instrument.
Bianca
Where left we last?
Lucentio
Here, madam:
    [*reading*] 'Hic ibat Simois, hic est Sigeia tellus,
Hic steterat Priami regia celsa senis.'
Bianca
30 Conster them.
Lucentio
'Hic ibat', as I told you before; 'Simois', I am Lucentio; 'hic est', son unto Vincentio of Pisa; 'Sigeia tellus', disguised thus to get your love; 'Hic steterat', and that Lucentio that comes a-wooing; 'Priami', is my man
35 Tranio; 'regia', bearing my port; 'celsa senis', that we might beguile the old pantaloon.
Hortensio
Madam, my instrument's in tune.
Bianca
Let's hear. [*He plays*] O fie, the treble jars!
Lucentio
Spit in the hole, man, and tune again.
Bianca
40 [*To* Lucentio] Now let me see if I can conster it. 'Hic ibat Simois', I know you not; 'hic est Sigeia tellus', I trust you not; 'Hic steterat Priami', take heed he hear us not; 'regia', presume not; 'celsa senis', despair not.
Hortensio
Madam, 'tis now in tune.
    [*He plays again*]
Lucentio   All but the bass.
Hortensio
45 The bass is right, 'tis the base knave that jars.
    [*Aside*] How fiery and forward our pedant is!
Now, for my life, the knave doth court my love.
Pedascule, I'll watch you better yet.
Bianca
[*To* Lucentio] In time I may believe, yet I mistrust.

45 *the bass*: the bass string on the lute; but
   Hortensio takes up the word and makes a
   suspicious pun.
48 *Pedascule*: A contemptuous dismissal (in a
   word coined for the purpose), of the 'little
   pedant'.
49 *yet*: at present.
50–51 Lucentio pretends to be discussing
   the translation of the next words from
   Ovid, *illic Aeacides*. He is correct in
   saying that this name belonged to the
   warrior Ajax — but Bianca is also right to
   question him: Aeacides was also the name
   of Achilles, who had the same
   grandfather, Aeacus.
56 *pleasant*: merry.
57 *give me leave*: leave me alone.

60 *withal*: as well.
   but: unless.

63 *order*: method.
64 *begin . . . art*: begin at the very beginning.
65 *gamut*: the musical scale.

68 *fairly drawn*: completely written out.

71 *ground*: basis.
   accord: harmony.
71–6 Hortensio's paper explains his love with
   the musical scale as systematized by
   Guido d'Arezzo in the eleventh century
   and called 'Gamma ut'.

78 *nice*: fussy.

Lucentio

50 [*Aside to* Bianca] Mistrust it not — [*Aloud*] for,
   sure, Aeacides
Was Ajax, called so from his grandfather.

Bianca

I must believe my master; else, I promise you,
I should be arguing still upon that doubt,
But let it rest. — Now, Litio, to you:
55 Good master, take it not unkindly, pray,
That I have been thus pleasant with you both.

Hortensio

[*To* Lucentio] You may go walk, and give me
   leave awhile:
My lessons make no music in three parts.

Lucentio

Are you so formal, sir? Well, I must wait—
60 [*Aside*] And watch withal, for, but I be
   deceived,
Our fine musician groweth amorous.

He stands aside

Hortensio

Madam, before you touch the instrument,
To learn the order of my fingering,
I must begin with rudiments of art,
65 To teach you gamut in a briefer sort,
More pleasant, pithy, and effectual,
Than hath been taught by any of my trade,
And there it is in writing fairly drawn.

Bianca

Why, I am past my gamut long ago.

Hortensio

70 Yet read the gamut of Hortensio.

Bianca

[*Reads*] 'Gamut, I am the ground of all accord;
A re, to plead Hortensio's passion;
B mi, Bianca, take him for thy lord
C fa ut, that loves with all affection;
75 *D sol re*, one clef, two notes have I;
E la mi, show pity or I die.'
Call you this 'gamut'? Tut, I like it not;
Old fashions please me best; I am not so nice
To change true rules for odd inventions.

Enter a Servant

Servant

80   Mistress, your father prays you leave your books
And help to dress your sister's chamber up.
You know tomorrow is the wedding-day.

Bianca

Farewell, sweet masters both, I must be gone.

[*Exeunt* Bianca *and* Servant.

Lucentio

Faith, mistress, then I have no cause to stay.

[*Exit*

Hortensio

85   But I have cause to pry into this pedant:
Methinks he looks as though he were in love.
Yet if thy thoughts, Bianca, be so humble
To cast thy wandering eyes on every stale,
Seize thee that list; if once I find thee ranging,

90   Hortensio will be quit with thee by changing.

[*Exit*

88   *stale*: decoy-bird.
89   *Seize thee that list*: anyone can have you.
ranging: straying.
90   *be quit*: get even.

Act 3   Scene 2

The wedding-day has arrived — but there is no
bridegroom. Katherina is very distressed, and
her father is sympathetic. Biondello brings
news of Petruchio's approach, describing what
cannot be seen on stage — the worn-out horse
— and preparing us for his master's fantastic
dress. Petruchio makes his entrance, and insists
on carrying Katherina off to the church to be
married. Tranio and Lucentio remain onstage,
discussing their plans for Bianca, until Gremio
returns and tells them of Petruchio's behaviour
in the church. When the wedding-party comes
back, Petruchio announces that he must leave
immediately — and take his new wife with
him. Katherina refuses: but Petruchio is
adamant.

Scene 2

Enter Baptista, Gremio, Tranio (*as*
Lucentio), Katherina, Bianca, Lucentio
(*as* Cambio) *and* attendants

Baptista

[*To* Tranio] Signor Lucentio, this is the 'pointed day
That Katherine and Petruchio should be married,
And yet we hear not of our son-in-law.
What will be said, what mockery will it be

5   To want the bridegroom when the priest attends
To speak the ceremonial rites of marriage?
What says Lucentio to this shame of ours?

1   *'pointed*: appointed.
3   *hear not*: have no news of.
5   *want*: lack.
8   *forsooth be forced*: Katherina considers this forced marriage to be in fact ('forsooth') a kind of rape.
9   *opposed . . . heart*: against my will.
10 *rudesby*: lout.
    full of spleen: intemperate: the spleen was thought to be the seat of both melancholic depression and excitability.
11 Katherina adapts the proverb, 'Marry in haste and repent at leisure'.
14 *to be noted for*: to get a reputation as.
15 *'point*: fix.
16 *Make . . . friends*: The text of the First Folio reads 'Make friends, invite' — which is neither metrical nor sensible; most modern editors accept this emendation, first proposed by Alexander Dyce.
    proclaim the banns: See note to 2, 1, 181.
21 Tranio suddenly becomes very familiar with Petruchio; this and subsequent speeches would come better from Hortensio, but he (in his disguise as Litio) has just left the stage.
22 *means but well*: has only the best intentions.
23 *fortune*: chance, accident.
    stays . . . word: stops him keeping his word.
24 *passing*: exceedingly.
25 *be merry*: jokes a lot.
    withal: at the same time.
26 *Would*: I wish.
28 *a very saint*: even a saint.
29 *humour*: temper.
30 *old*: rare, strange; the word is absent from the Folio text (where Biondello says simply 'such news'), but Baptista's response — taking the word in a different sense — in the next line demands 'old' here.

Katherina

No shame but mine, I must forsooth be forced
To give my hand, opposed against my heart,
10 Unto a mad-brain rudesby, full of spleen,
Who wooed in haste and means to wed at leisure.
I told you, I, he was a frantic fool,
Hiding his bitter jests in blunt behaviour;
And to be noted for a merry man,
15 He'll woo a thousand, 'point the day of marriage,
Make feast, invite friends and proclaim the banns,
Yet never means to wed where he hath wooed.
Now must the world point at poor Katherine
And say 'Lo, there is mad Petruchio's wife,
20 If it would please him come and marry her'.

Tranio

Patience, good Katherine, and Baptista too.
Upon my life, Petruchio means but well,
Whatever fortune stays him from his word.
Though he be blunt, I know him passing wise;
25 Though he be merry, yet withal he's honest.

Katherina

Would Katherine had never seen him though!

[*Exit weeping*

Baptista

Go, girl, I cannot blame thee now to weep,
For such an injury would vex a very saint,
Much more a shrew of thy impatient humour.

Enter Biondello

Biondello

30 Master, master, news, and such old news as you never heard of!

Baptista

Is it new and old too? How may that be?

Biondello

Why, is it not news to hear of Petruchio's coming?

Baptista

Is he come?

Biondello

35 Why, no, sir.

Baptista

What then?

Biondello

He is coming.

40 *what to*: what about.
   old: Tranio reverts to Biondello's usage,
   giving a cue for the prose description
   which must be spoken very quickly,
   especially when Biondello lists the horse's
   ailments in terms which, though they are
   all correct, would probably be as familiar
   to the original hearers — both on stage
   and in the audience — as an account of
   the mechanical failings of a second-hand
   car.
42 *jerkin*: jacket.
   turned: turned inside out.
43 *candle-cases*: used to keep candle-ends in
   (having already been discarded).
45 *chapeless*: without the chape — the metal
   covering on the scabbard which protects
   the point of the sword.
46 *two broken points*: jagged edges; 'points'
   are also the laces which would fasten
   Petruchio's breeches — but Biondello is
   no longer describing clothing.
   hipped: with a dislocated hip.
   mothy: moth-eaten.
47 *of no kindred*: unrelated, not like each
   other.
   possessed: afflicted; Biondello's catalogue
   of equine diseases mixes technical terms
   with dialectal variants.

Baptista
When will he be here?
   Biondello
When he stands where I am and sees you there.
   Tranio
40 But say, what to thine old news?
   Biondello
Why, Petruchio is coming in a new hat and an old
jerkin; a pair of old breeches thrice turned; a pair of
boots that have been candle-cases, one buckled,
another laced; an old rusty sword ta'en out of the town
45 armoury, with a broken hilt, and chapeless; with two
broken points; his horse hipped, with an old mothy
saddle and stirrups of no kindred; besides, possessed

48 *glanders*: contagious disease whose
   symptoms are a nasal discharge and a
   swelling beneath the jaw.
   like to: liable to.
   mose in the chine: crumble in the spine.
49 *lampass*: disease causing swelling in the
   mouth and a film-like growth over the
   teeth.
   fashions: farcin, a disease similar to
   glanders.
50 *windgalls*: soft tumours in the leg, just
   above the fetlock.

with the glanders and like to mose in the chine,
troubled with the lampass, infected with the fashions,
50 full of windgalls, sped with spavins, rayed with the
yellows, past cure of the fives, stark spoiled with the
staggers, begnawn with the bots, swayed in the back
and shoulder-shotten, near-legged before, and with a
half-cheeked bit and a headstall of sheep's leather
55 which, being restrained to keep him from stumbling,
hath been often burst, and new-repaired with knots;

sped: ruined.

spavins: swollen leg-joints.

rayed: disfigured.

yellows: jaundice.

51 *past cure*: incurable.

the fives: vives, growths beneath the ear.

stark: absolutely.

staggers: any disease which affected movement.

52 *begnawn with the bots*: eaten away with worms.

swayed in the back: sway-backed.

53 *shoulder-shotten*: with dislocated shoulder.

near-legged before: knock-kneed in front.

54 *half-cheeked bit*: bridle with an improperly adjusted bit.

headstall: part of bridle fitting over horse's head.

sheep's leather: i.e. a cheaper leather, not so strong as cowhide.

55 *being restrained*: tightened (by pulling on the reins).

56 *new-repaired*: mended again.

girth: the strap from the saddle going under the horse's belly.

57 *pieced*: patched.

crupper: the strap which passes under the horse's tail to stop the saddle from slipping forwards.

velour: velvet-like fabric (probably a cover for the crupper).

58–9 *two . . . studs*: her initials clearly marked with studs.

59 *pieced*: mended.

pack-thread: string (for tying parcels).

62 *lackey*: footman.

for all the world: in every respect.

caparisoned: decked out.

63 *stock*: stocking.

kersey boot-hose: over-stocking (worn under the riding-boot) made from coarse woollen fabric.

64 *list*: strip of cloth made from the cut-off selvage of a length of fabric.

65–6 *humour . . . feather*: No-one knows the exact meaning of this phrase; I would suggest that the hat is decorated with a bunch of ribbons pinned on in place of a feather.

humour: sort of.

forty: any large number — 'lots of'.

fancies: notions.

pricked in't: pinned on.

67 *Christian footboy*: decent page.

---

one girth six times pieced, and a woman's crupper of velour, which hath two letters for her name fairly set down in studs, and here and there pieced with pack- 60 thread.

Baptista

Who comes with him?

Biondello

O sir, his lackey, for all the world caparisoned like the horse: with a linen stock on one leg and a kersey boot-hose on the other, gartered with a red and blue list; an 65 old hat, and the humour of forty fancies pricked in't for a feather; a monster, a very monster in apparel, and not like a Christian footboy or a gentleman's lackey.

Tranio

'Tis some odd humour pricks him to the fashion, Yet oftentimes he goes but mean-apparelled.

Baptista

70 I am glad he's come, howsoe'er he comes.

Biondello

Why, sir, he comes not.

Baptista

Didst thou not say he comes?

Biondello

Who? That Petruchio came?

Baptista

Ay, that Petruchio came?

Biondello

75 No, sir, I say his horse comes with him on his back.

Baptista

Why, that's all one.

Biondello

    Nay, by Saint Jamy,
    I hold you a penny,
    A horse and a man
80   Is more than one,
    And yet not many.

Enter Petruchio *and* Grumio

Petruchio

Come, where be these gallants? Who's at home?

Baptista

You are welcome, sir.

68 *humour*: mood.
   pricks: urges, incites.
69 *oftentimes*: frequently.
   but: only.
   mean: poorly.
76 *all one*: the same thing.
77 *Saint Jamy*: St. James; there is no known source for Biondello's rhyme.
78 *hold*: bet.
81 *many*: a company ('meiny').
82 *be*: are.
   gallants: lads.
84 *not well*: i.e. not well-dressed.
85 *halt not*: are not lame.
89 *Gentles*: gentlefolk; Petruchio addresses the assembled company with excessive — old-fashioned — courtesy.
   methinks: it seems to me that.
90 *goodly*: worthy.
91 *monument*: omen.
92 *comet*: Comets were thought to be warnings of disaster.
   prodigy: portent.
95 *unprovided*: unprepared.
96 *doff this habit*: take off these clothes.
   shame to your estate: a disgrace for a man in your position.
97 *solemn festival*: ceremonies.
98 *occasion of import*: important matter.
99 *all so long*: for so very long.
102 *Sufficeth*: let it be enough.
103 *digress*: change my plans.

107 *wears*: is passing.

108 *unreverent*: disrespectful.

112 *Good sooth*: yes indeed.
    ha' done with: that's enough of.

Petruchio
And yet I come not well?
Baptista
85 And yet you halt not.
Tranio
Not so well apparelled as I wish you were.
Petruchio
Were it not better I should rush in thus?
But where is Kate? Where is my lovely bride?
How does my father? Gentles, methinks you frown,
90 And wherefore gaze this goodly company
As if they saw some wondrous monument,
Some comet, or unusual prodigy?
Baptista
Why, sir, you know this is your wedding-day.
First were we sad, fearing you would not come,
95 Now sadder, that you come so unprovided.
Fie, doff this habit, shame to your estate,
An eyesore to our solemn festival!
Tranio
And tell us what occasion of import
Hath all so long detained you from your wife
100 And sent you hither so unlike yourself.
Petruchio
Tedious it were to tell, and harsh to hear.
Sufficeth I am come to keep my word,
Though in some part enforcèd to digress,
Which at more leisure I will so excuse
105 As you shall well be satisfied with all.
But where is Kate? I stay too long from her,
The morning wears, 'tis time we were at church.
Tranio
See not your bride in these unreverent robes,
Go to my chamber, put on clothes of mine.
Petruchio
110 Not I, believe me; thus I'll visit her.
Baptista
But thus, I trust, you will not marry her.
Petruchio
Good sooth, even thus. Therefore ha' done with words;
To me she's married, not unto my clothes.

114 *wear*: wear out — i.e. by sexually
    exhausting him.
115 *accoutrements*: attire.

119 *lovely*: loving.

120 *meaning in*: reason for.

123 *I'll after*: I'll go after.
    event: outcome.

124 *to love*: i.e. to Lucentio's love for Bianca.
    Tranio has apparently told Lucentio of
    his success with Bianca.
    concerneth us: it is in our interests.
125 *liking*: approval.
    bring to pass: achieve.
126 *As before imparted*: as I said before.
128 *skills not much*: doesn't matter much.
    fit . . . turn: make him serve our purpose.
130 *make assurance*: guarantee.
132 *enjoy your hope*: achieve what you have
    been hoping for.
133 *with consent*: i.e. her father's consent.

135 *steps*: movements.
    narrowly: closely.
136 *steal our marriage*: get married secretly.
137 *say no*: forbid it.

139 'We'll do it gradually.'
140 *watch our vantage*: wait for an
    opportunity.
141 *overreach*: out-do, beat.
142 *narrow-prying*: closely watching.
143 *quaint*: ingenious, crafty.
144 *Lucentio*: Tranio's speech is addressed to
    the audience, pointing out the direction in
    which this complicated plot is moving.

145 *Gremio*: The church service has not taken
    long.

Could I repair what she will wear in me
115 As I can change these poor accoutrements,
'Twere well for Kate and better for myself.
But what a fool am I to chat with you,
When I should bid good morrow to my bride,
And seal the title with a lovely kiss!
                    [*Exeunt* Petruchio *and* Grumio

Tranio
120 He hath some meaning in his mad attire.
We will persuade him, be it possible,
To put on better ere he go to church.

Baptista
I'll after him and see the event of this.
                [*Exeunt all except* Tranio *and* Lucentio

Tranio
But, sir, to love concerneth us to add
125 Her father's liking, which to bring to pass,
As before imparted to your worship,
I am to get a man, whate'er he be—
It skills not much, we'll fit him to our turn—
And he shall be Vincentio of Pisa,
130 And make assurance here in Padua
Of greater sums than I have promised.
So shall you quietly enjoy your hope
And marry sweet Bianca with consent.

Lucentio
Were it not that my fellow schoolmaster
135 Doth watch Bianca's steps so narrowly,
'Twere good methinks to steal our marriage,
Which once performed, let all the world say no,
I'll keep mine own despite of all the world.

Tranio
That by degrees we mean to look into,
140 And watch our vantage in this business.
We'll overreach the greybeard Gremio,
The narrow-prying father Minola,
The quaint musician, amorous Litio,
All for my master's sake, Lucentio.

Enter Gremio

145 Signor Gremio, came you from the church?

Gremio
As willingly as e'er I came from school.

147 *is*: are; Shakespeare often uses a singular
verb when two singular nouns form the
subject.

Tranio
And is the bride and bridegroom coming home?

148 *a groom indeed*: a real groom — i.e. a
peasant.

150 *Curster*: more curst.

152 *the devil's dam*: the devil's mother — who
was worse than her son.

153 *fool*: harmless innocent.
to: compared to.
154 *Sir Lucentio*: Gremio speaks politely.
155 *Should ask*: came to the point (in the
marriage service) where he is required to
ask Petruchio.
156 *by gog's wouns*: by God's (Christ's)
wounds; a fairly common oath at this
time.
159 *took . . . cuff*: gave him such a blow.
161 *if any list*: if anybody wants to.

Gremio
A bridegroom, say you? 'Tis a groom indeed,
A grumbling groom, and that the girl shall find.
Tranio
150 Curster than she? Why, 'tis impossible.
Gremio
Why, he's a devil, a devil, a very fiend.
Tranio
Why, she's a devil, a devil, the devil's dam.
Gremio
Tut, she's a lamb, a dove, a fool to him.
I'll tell you, Sir Lucentio: when the priest
155 Should ask if Katherine should be his wife,
'Ay, by gog's wouns', quoth he, and swore so loud
That all-amazed the priest let fall the book,
And as he stooped again to take it up,
This mad-brained bridegroom took him such a cuff
160 That down fell priest and book, and book and priest.
'Now take them up', quoth he, 'if any list.'

Tranio
What said the wench when he rose up again?
Gremio
Trembled and shook; for why, he stamped and swore
As if the vicar meant to cozen him.

163 *for why*: on account of which.
164 *cozen*: cheat.
165 *after . . . done*: when all the religious rites were finished.

165 But after many ceremonies done
He calls for wine. 'A health!' quoth he, as if
He had been aboard, carousing to his mates

167 *aboard*: on board ship.
carousing: drinking healths.
168 *the muscadel*: At the end of the Elizabethan wedding ceremony, it was customary for the bride to put cakes — 'sops' — into a cup of sweet wine — 'muscatel' — which was shared by the entire wedding party.

After a storm; quaffed off the muscadel,
And threw the sops all in the sexton's face,
170 Having no other reason
But that his beard grew thin and hungerly
And seemed to ask him sops as he was drinking.

171 *hungerly*: sparsely, hungrily.
172 *ask him sops*: ask him for the sops.

This done, he took the bride about the neck,
And kissed her lips with such a clamorous smack
175 That at the parting all the church did echo;
And I, seeing this, came thence for very shame,
And after me, I know, the rout is coming.
Such a mad marriage never was before.

177 *the rout*: the whole crowd of guests.

Music plays

Hark, hark, I hear the minstrels play.

Enter Petruchio, Katherina, Bianca, Hortensio, Baptista, Grumio, *and* Attendants

Petruchio

180 *pains*: concern.
181 *think*: expect.
182 *cheer*: food and drink.
183 *my haste . . . hence*: I am in a hurry to get away.

180 Gentlemen and friends, I thank you for your pains.
I know you think to dine with me today,
And have prepared great store of wedding cheer,
But so it is, my haste doth call me hence,
And therefore here I mean to take my leave.
Baptista
185 Is't possible you will away tonight?
Petruchio
I must away today before night come.

185 *will away*: will go away.

Make it no wonder: if you knew my business,
You would entreat me rather go than stay.
And, honest company, I thank you all

186 *must away*: must go away.
187 *Make it no wonder*: don't be surprised.

190 That have beheld me give away myself
To this most patient, sweet, and virtuous wife.
Dine with my father, drink a health to me,
For I must hence, and farewell to you all.

Tranio

195 Let us entreat you stay till after dinner.

Petruchio

It may not be.

Gremio

                    Let me entreat you.

Petruchio

It cannot be.

Katherina

                    Let me entreat you.

Petruchio

200 I am content.

Katherina

                    Are you content to stay?

Petruchio

I am content you shall entreat me stay—

But yet not stay, entreat me how you can.

Katherina

Now if you love me, stay.

Petruchio

205   Grumio, my horse.

Grumio

Ay, sir, they be ready, the oats have eaten the

horses.

Katherina

Nay then, do what thou canst, I will not go today,

No, nor tomorrow, not till I please myself.

210 The door is open, sir, there lies your way,

You may be jogging whiles your boots are green.

For me, I'll not be gone till I please myself.

'Tis like you'll prove a jolly surly groom

That take it on you at the first so roundly.

Petruchio

215 O Kate, content thee, prithee be not angry.

Katherina

I will be angry; what hast thou to do?

—Father, be quiet; he shall stay my leisure.

Gremio

Ay marry, sir, now it begins to work.

Katherina

Gentlemen, forward to the bridal dinner.

220 I see a woman may be made a fool

If she had not a spirit to resist.

205 *horse*: As a plural form (like *sheep* and *deer*) *horse* was available until the 17th century.

206-7 *oats . . . horses*: Grumio's nonsense might be taken to mean that the feed was stronger than Petruchio's poor animals.

211 A proverbial saying, meaning 'go while you can'.
green: fresh.

213 *jolly*: arrogant.
groom: See note on line 148.

214 *take it on you*: presume.
roundly: boldly.

216 *what . . . to do*: what has it to do with you.

217 *Father, be quiet*: Katherina anticipates an interruption from Baptista.
stay my leisure: wait until I am ready.

218 *now . . . work*: things are beginning to happen now.

Petruchio

They shall go forward, Kate, at thy command.
—Obey the bride, you that attend on her.
Go to the feast, revel and domineer,
225 Carouse full measure to her maidenhead,
Be mad and merry, or go hang yourselves;
But for my bonny Kate, she must with me.
Nay, look not big, nor stamp, nor stare, nor fret,
I will be master of what is mine own.
230 She is my goods, my chattels, she is my house,
My household stuff, my field, my barn,
My horse, my ox, my ass, my any thing,
And here she stands, touch her whoever dare!
I'll bring mine action on the proudest he
235 That stops my way in Padua. — Grumio,
Draw forth thy weapon, we are beset with thieves,
Rescue thy mistress if thou be a man.
—Fear not, sweet wench, they shall not touch thee, Kate;
I'll buckler thee against a million.

[*Exeunt* Petruchio, Katherina, *and* Grumio

Baptista

240 Nay, let them go, a couple of quiet ones.

Gremio

Went they not quickly, I should die with laughing.

Tranio

Of all mad matches never was the like.

Lucentio

Mistress, what's your opinion of your sister?

Bianca

That being mad herself, she's madly mated.

Gremio

245 I warrant him, Petruchio is Kated.

Baptista

Neighbours and friends, though bride and
        bridegroom wants
For to supply the places at the table,
You know there wants no junkets at the feast.
Lucentio, you shall supply the bridegroom's place,
250 And let Bianca take her sister's room.

Tranio

Shall sweet Bianca practise how to bride it?

Baptista

She shall, Lucentio. Come, gentlemen, let's go.

[*Exeunt*

---

224 *domineer*: riot.
225 *full measure*: all you can.
227 *must*: must go; Petruchio is pretending that he must protect Katherina from the noisy revellers.
228 *look not big*: don't defy me; Petruchio speaks to the onlookers — who are making no resistance.
       stare: look round wildly.
230-2 Petruchio seems to refer to the Tenth Commandment, which prohibits covetousness.
230 *chattels*: moveable possessions.
231 *household stuff*: furniture.
234 *bring mine action*: take legal proceedings against.
       he: man.

239 *buckler*: defend, shield.

241 *Went they not*: if they had not gone.

244 *madly mated*: matched with a madman.

245 *Kated*: matched with Kate.

246 *wants*: are missing.

247 *supply the places*: take their places.
249 *there wants no*: there is no lack of.
       junkets: sweetmeats, delicacies.

250 *room*: seat.

251 *to bride it*: to act like a bride; Tranio seems to step back into his assumed role as the lover of Bianca, and Baptista recognizes him as 'Lucentio'.

Act 4

Grumio has returned, ahead of his master, to
Petruchio's home. He tells the servants about
their new mistress, Katherina, and recounts the
horrors of their journey from Padua. Grumio
instructs the servingmen about the reception
they must give to the newly-married couple,
and this comical episode prepares the audience
for the arrival of Petruchio, who enters in a
rage and starts abusing his servants. Katherina
speaks very little: she is tired, and frightened.
When she has gone to bed, Petruchio addresses
the audience with one of the most important
speeches in the play. He describes the method
he will use for taming his shrew — and an
Elizabethan audience would know that this is
the recognized method of taming and training a
hawk.

 1 *jades*: nags, weak horses.
 2 *ways*: roads.
 3 *rayed*: muddied.
    am sent before: have been sent ahead.
 5 *a little pot*: Grumio is apparently small in
    stature; he refers to a proverbial saying
    that a small pot boils quickly (i.e. a little
    person easily gets angry).
 7 *come by*: find.
 8 *blowing the fire*: fanning the embers; there
    was a proverbial saying, 'Let him that is
    a-cold blow at the coal'.
 9 *taller*: stronger (as well as bigger).
    take: catch.
10 *Curtis*: This seems a strange name for an
    Italian servant; it was, in fact, the name
    of an actor who played small parts in
    Shakespeare's company.
13 *no greater a run*: i.e. to get up speed.
16–17 *fire . . . water*: An adaptation of a
    popular catch 'Scotland's burning . . .
    Fire, fire! Cast on water!'; Grumio needs
    fire, not water.
18 *hot*: intense.

Scene 1

Enter Grumio

Grumio

Fie, fie on all tired jades, on all mad masters, and all
foul ways! Was ever man so beaten? Was ever man so
rayed? Was ever man so weary? I am sent before to
make a fire, and they are coming after to warm them.
5 Now were not I a little pot and soon hot, my very lips
might freeze to my teeth, my tongue to the roof of my
mouth, my heart in my belly, ere I should come by a
fire to thaw me; but I with blowing the fire shall warm
myself, for, considering the weather, a taller man than
10 I will take cold. Holla, ho, Curtis!

Enter Curtis

Curtis

Who is that calls so coldly?

Grumio

A piece of ice. If thou doubt it, thou mayst slide from
my shoulder to my heel with no greater a run but my
head and my neck. A fire, good Curtis.

Curtis

15 Is my master and his wife coming, Grumio?

Grumio

O ay, Curtis, ay — and therefore fire, fire, cast on no
water.

Curtis

Is she so hot a shrew as she's reported?

Grumio

She was, good Curtis, before this frost; but thou
20 know'st winter tames man, woman, and beast: for it
hath tamed my old master, and my new mistress, and
myself, fellow Curtis.

20 *winter . . . beast*: The proverb is 'Winter and wedlock tame both man and beast'.
22 *fellow Curtis*: Grumio allows Curtis to identify himself as his 'fellow' — and by implication a beast.
23 *three-inch fool*: little fool; Curtis alludes only to Grumio's height, but Grumio takes it in another sense.
24 *thy horn*: Grumio refers to the horn that was said to grow from a cuckold's forehead; he claims to equal its length — the implication being that it is he who cuckolded Curtis.
28 *cold comfort*: discomfort.
   hot office: job of making a fire.
29 *how goes the world*: what's the news.
31 *have thy duty*: i.e. take what is due to you.

35 *Jack boy, ho boy*: Another popular song or catch.

37 *cony-catching*: trickery — with some play on Grumio's fondness for catches.

39 *trimmed*: tidied.
40 *rushes*: the normal floor-covering.
41 *fustian*: coarse (and cheap) fabric, suitable for servingmen's livery.
   their: Folio 1 reads 'the'.
42 *wedding-garment*: This may be no more than a token, like the carnation worn nowadays; but see St Matthew 22:12.
   jacks: lads; *also* containers, often made of leather, for liquor — which could be mouldy inside.
   jills: lasses; *also* drinking-vessels made of metal — and likely to need polishing.
43 *without*: outside.
   carpets: woollen tablecloths.

50 *thereby hangs a tale*: there's a good story about that.

51 *ha't*: have it.

Curtis
Away, you three-inch fool, I am no beast.
Grumio
Am I but three inches? Why, thy horn is a foot, and so
25 long am I at the least. But wilt thou make a fire, or shall I complain on thee to our mistress, whose hand — she being now at hand — thou shalt soon feel, to thy cold comfort, for being slow in thy hot office?
Curtis
I prithee, good Grumio, tell me how goes the world?
Grumio
30 A cold world, Curtis, in every office but thine — and therefore fire. Do thy duty, and have thy duty, for my master and mistress are almost frozen to death.
Curtis
There's fire ready, and therefore, good Grumio, the news.
Grumio
35 Why, 'Jack boy, ho boy!' and as much news as wilt thou.
Curtis
Come, you are so full of cony-catching.
Grumio
Why therefore fire, for I have caught extreme cold. Where's the cook, is supper ready, the house trimmed,
40 rushes strewed, cobwebs swept, the servingmen in their new fustian, their white stockings, and every officer his wedding-garment on? Be the jacks fair within, the jills fair without, the carpets laid, and everything in order?
Curtis
45 All ready, and therefore, I pray thee, news.
Grumio
First, know my horse is tired, my master and mistress fallen out.
Curtis
How?
Grumio
Out of their saddles into the dirt, and thereby hangs a
50 tale.
Curtis
Let's ha't, good Grumio.

52 *Lend thine ear*: listen.

56 *sensible*: capable of being felt —
   appreciated by the sense;
   also reasonable, easily understood.
58 *Inprimis*: first of all; Grumio attempts
   legal jargon.

60 *of*: on.

63 *crossed*: interrupted.

65 *miry*: muddy.
66 *bemoiled*: covered in mud.

72 *of worthy memory*: worth recording.
73 *unexperienced*: ignorant.
75 *By this reckoning*: from this account.
   more shrew: more of a shrew; the word is
   applicable to either sex.
77 *what*: why.
79 *and the rest*: Shakespeare probably did not
   know which, or how many, actors would
   be available to play these servingmen.
   slickly: sleekly.
80 *blue coats*: normal servant uniform.
81 *indifferent*: alike, matching.
   left legs: a sign of respect; to curtsy, or
   bow, with the right leg was a gesture of
   defiance.
83 *kiss their hands*: an elaborately courteous
   gesture.

Grumio

Lend thine ear.

Curtis

Here.

Grumio

[*Cuffing him*] There.

Curtis

55 This 'tis to feel a tale, not to hear a tale.

Grumio

And therefore 'tis called a sensible tale; and this cuff
was but to knock at your ear and beseech listening.
Now I begin. *Inprimis* we came down a foul hill, my
master riding behind my mistress—

Curtis

60 Both of one horse?

Grumio

What's that to thee?

Curtis

Why, a horse.

Grumio

Tell thou the tale. But hadst thou not crossed me, thou
shouldst have heard how her horse fell, and she under
65 her horse; thou shouldst have heard in how miry a
place, how she was bemoiled, how he left her with the
horse upon her, how he beat me because her horse
stumbled, how she waded through the dirt to pluck
him off me; how he swore, how she prayed, that never
70 prayed before; how I cried, how the horses ran away,
how her bridle was burst; how I lost my crupper —
with many things of worthy memory, which now shall
die in oblivion, and thou return unexperienced to thy
grave.

Curtis

75 By this reckoning he is more shrew than she.

Grumio

Ay, and that thou and the proudest of you all shall find
when he comes home. But what talk I of this? Call
forth Nathaniel, Joseph, Nicholas, Philip, Walter,
Sugarsop, and the rest. Let their heads be slickly
80 combed, their blue coats brushed, and their garters of
an indifferent knit; let them curtsy with their left legs,
and not presume to touch a hair of my master's horse-
tail till they kiss their hands. Are they all ready?

Curtis
They are.

Grumio
85 Call them forth.

Curtis
Do you hear, ho? You must meet my master to
countenance my mistress.

Grumio
Why, she hath a face of her own.

Curtis
Who knows not that?

Grumio
90 Thou, it seems, that calls for company to countenance
her.

Curtis
I call them forth to credit her.

Enter four or five Servingmen

Grumio
Why, she comes to borrow nothing of them.

Nathaniel
Welcome home, Grumio.

Philip
95 How now, Grumio

Joseph
What, Grumio.

Nicholas
Fellow Grumio.

Nathaniel
How now, old lad.

Grumio
Welcome, you! — How now, you! — What, you! —
100 Fellow you! And thus much for greeting. Now, my
spruce companions, is all ready, and all things neat?

Nathaniel
All things is ready. How near is our master?

Grumio
E'en at hand, alighted by this; and therefore be not —
Cock's passion, silence, I hear my master.

Enter Petruchio *and* Katherina

87 *countenance*: to pay respect to; Grumio, of course, wilfully misunderstands.

92 *credit*: honour; Grumio chooses to understand 'offer financial credit'.
92s.d. *four or five*: Shakespeare asks again — as at *4, 1, 79* — for whatever actors are available.

101 *spruce companions*: fine fellows.
neat: tidy.

103 *E'en at hand*: very close indeed.
alighted: dismounted.
104 *Cock's passion*: God's (i.e. Christ's) suffering.

105 *at door*: to open the door.
106 *hold my stirrup*: i.e. to keep it steady whilst the rider dismounted.

Petruchio
105 Where be these knaves? What, no man at door
To hold my stirrup nor to take my horse?
Where is Nathaniel, Gregory, Philip?
All Servingmen
Here, here sir, here sir.
Petruchio
'Here sir, here sir, here sir, here sir'!

110 *logger-headed*: block-headed; Petruchio has a fine command of abusive terms.
111 *regard*: respect.
duty: obedience.

110 You logger-headed and unpolished grooms!
What? No attendance? No regard? No duty?
Where is the foolish knave I sent before?
Grumio
Here sir, as foolish as I was before.
Petruchio
You peasant swain, you whoreson malt-horse
    drudge,

114 *peasant swain*: country oaf.
whoreson: son of a whore.
malt-horse: heavy horse turning a treadmill to grind malt; the epitome of mindless drudgery.
115 *meet me in the park*: i.e. before the party arrived at the house.
118 *pumps . . . heel*: light shoes, whose heels should have been decorated with a pattern of small holes (pinked); Grumio is inventing excuses — in a manner (and in verse) which suggests that he is an accomplice in Petruchio's scheme.
119 *link*: torch, whose smoke could be used to darken the hat.
120 *sheathing*: being fitted with a sheath.
121 *fine*: properly dressed.

115 Did I not bid thee meet me in the park
And bring along these rascal knaves with thee?
Grumio
Nathaniel's coat, sir, was not fully made,
And Gabriel's pumps were all unpinked i'th'heel;
There was no link to colour Peter's hat,
120 And Walter's dagger was not come from sheathing;
There were none fine but Adam, Ralph, and
    Gregory,
The rest were ragged, old, and beggarly,
Yet, as they are, here are they come to meet you.
Petruchio
Go, rascals, go and fetch my supper in.
                    [*Exeunt* Servingmen

125-6 Petruchio sings an old ballad.

125   *Where is the life that late I led?*
        Where are those —
    Sit down, Kate, and welcome. Food, food, food,
    food

128 *Why, when*: Exclamations of impatience.

Why, when, I say!

                Enter Servants *with supper*

Nay, good sweet Kate, be merry.

131-32 The opening words of a ballad.

130 —Off with my boots, you rogues — you villains,
    when!

                Servant attends to his boot

It was a friar of orders grey,
As he forth walkèd on his way —

133 *pluck . . . awry*: pull my foot the wrong
way (as the servant pulls off his boot).

134 *mend*: improve.

Out you rogue! You pluck my foot awry.
Take that [*He kicks the* Servant] and mend the
  plucking of the other.

135 —Be merry, Kate. — Some water here! What ho!

Enter one with water

136 *Troilus*: The name of a faithful lover in
Greek legend; spaniels are noted for
fidelity to their masters.

137 *cousin Ferdinand*: No such character ever
appears — and perhaps there is no need
for anyone to take notice of this order,
which is only part of the scheme to
confuse Katherina.

140 *wash*: i.e. wash your hands — fingers were
commonly used, with knives and spoons,
for eating.

Where's my spaniel Troilus? Sirrah, get you hence,
And bid my cousin Ferdinand come hither.
—One, Kate, that you must kiss and be acquainted
  with.
—Where are my slippers? Shall I have some water?
140 —Come, Kate, and wash, and welcome heartily.
—You whoreson villain, will you let it fall?

Katherina

Patience, I pray you, 'twas a fault unwilling.

Petruchio

143 *beetle-headed*: A 'beetle' was a heavy
mallet.
flap-eared: with flapping ears (like a
donkey).

144 *have a stomach*: are hungry.

145 *give thanks*: say grace.

A whoreson, beetle-headed, flap-eared knave!
—Come, Kate, sit down, I know you have a
  stomach.
145 Will you give thanks, sweet Kate, or else shall I?
—What's this? Mutton?

Servingman

Ay.

Petruchio

Who brought it?

Peter

I.

Petruchio

150 'Tis burnt, and so is all the meat.
What dogs are these! Where is the rascal cook?
How durst you, villains, bring it from the dresser

152 *dresser*: side table on which the food was
prepared.

And serve it thus to me that love it not?

He throws the food at them

154 *trenchers*: wooden plates.

155 *joltheads*: blockheads.

156 *be with you straight*: see to you at once.

There, take it to you, trenchers, cups, and all.
155 You heedless joltheads and unmannered slaves!
What, do you grumble? I'll be with you straight.
                                    [*Exeunt* Servants

Katherina

157 *disquiet*: distressed; Kate is already
somewhat subdued.

I pray you, husband, be not so disquiet.
The meat was well, if you were so contented.

160 *expressly*: especially.

161 *it engenders . . . anger*: It was generally thought that over-cooked meat produced an excess of the choleric humour, which caused anger.

163 *of ourselves*: naturally.

164 *it*: i.e. their choler.

165 *mended*: improved.

166 *for company*: together.

169 *kills . . . humour*: beats her at her own game — Petruchio's bad temper is defeating Katherina's temper; Peter should be speaking for the audience as they begin to recognize the 'taming' technique.

171 *of continency*: about self-control.

172 *rails*: shouts.
     rates: scolds.
     that: so that.

174 *new risen*: just woken up.

175 *Away, away*: It is essential that the stage should be cleared at this point, so that Petruchio's address is spoken directly to the audience, taking them into his confidence, and reminding them of the process of taming a hawk; compare Appendix p.104.

176 *politicly*: with cunning.

178 *sharp*: hungry.
     passing: exceedingly.

179 *stoop*: submit; in falconry, this term denotes the bird's sudden descent on to its prey.
     full-gorged: fully fed.

180 *then*: i.e. when she is fully fed.
     lure: artificial bird, made of feathers, with which the hawk is trained.

181 *man my haggard*: tame my wild (female) hawk.

182 *her keeper's call*: Each falconer has a distinct note for his bird.

183 *to watch her*: keep her awake.
     these kites: those wretched falcons.

184 *bate and beat*: rage and beat their wings with frustrated anger.

185 *meat*: food.

Petruchio
I tell thee, Kate, 'twas burnt and dried away,
160 And I expressly am forbid to touch it,
For it engenders choler, planteth anger,
And better 'twere that both of us did fast,
Since, of ourselves, ourselves are choleric,
Than feed it with such over-roasted flesh.
165 Be patient, tomorrow 't shall be mended,
And for this night we'll fast for company.
Come, I will bring thee to thy bridal chamber.
                                    [*Exeunt*

Enter Servants, *severally*

Nathaniel
Peter, didst ever see the like?
     Peter
He kills her in her own humour.

Enter Curtis

     Grumio
170 Where is he?
     Curtis   In her chamber.
Making a sermon of continency to her,
And rails, and swears, and rates, that she, poor soul,
Knows not which way to stand, to look, to speak,
And sits as one new risen from a dream.
175 Away, away, for he is coming hither.
                                    [*Exeunt*

Enter Petruchio

     Petruchio
Thus have I politicly begun my reign,
And 'tis my hope to end successfully.
My falcon now is sharp and passing empty,
And till she stoop she must not be full-gorged,
180 For then she never looks upon her lure.
Another way I have to man my haggard,
To make her come and know her keeper's call:
That is, to watch her, as we watch these kites
That bate and beat and will not be obedient.
185 She ate no meat today, nor none shall eat.
Last night she slept not, nor tonight she shall not.

191 *hurly*: commotion.
    intend: shall pretend.
192 *reverent*: respectful.
193 *watch*: stay awake.
194 *nod*: fall asleep.
    rail: shout.
    brawl: cause an uproar.
195 *still*: always.
196 *to . . . kindness*: Petruchio really means just the opposite of this proverbial utterance, referring to someone who is harmed by excessive care.
198 *shrew*: The word was clearly pronounced to rhyme with 'show'.
199 *'tis charity*: it would help everybody.

As with the meat, some undeservèd fault
I'll find about the making of the bed,
And here I'll fling the pillow, there the bolster,
190 This way the coverlet, another way the sheets.
Ay, and amid this hurly I intend
That all is done in reverent care of her.
And, in conclusion, she shall watch all night,
And if she chance to nod I'll rail and brawl,
195 And with the clamour keep her still awake.
This is a way to kill a wife with kindness,
And thus I'll curb her mad and headstrong humour.
He that knows better how to tame a shrew,
Now let him speak; 'tis charity to show.

[*Exit*

Act 4   Scene 2

The scene returns to Padua, where Hortensio (still disguised as the music-teacher, Litio) has told Tranio (disguised as Lucentio) that Bianca is in love with their rival. They stand aside to overhear Bianca and the real Lucentio declare their love for each other; and then together Hortensio and Tranio renounce their love for Bianca. Hortensio leaves the stage, vowing to wed a rich widow — and Tranio puts off his disguise and congratulates his old master and his new mistress on the success of their plot. Biondello brings news of the arrival of a stranger in town, and Tranio, practising a clever deception on the old man, induces him to play the part of Vincentio, the father of Lucentio.

2–3 *bears . . . hand*: is leading me on with false hopes.
4 *satisfy you in*: prove to you.
5 *mark*: note.
6 *read*: study; the two use this word in several senses as they come to their declaration of love.
7 *read*: teach.
    resolve me that: answer that for me.
8 *that I profess*: what I practise.
    The Art to Love: i.e. Ovid's *Ars Amatoria*.
9 *master of your art*: successful in your study; this reference to a university degree (M.A.) initiates a word-play in the following lines.

Scene 2

> *Enter* Tranio (*as* Lucentio), *and* Hortensio (*as* Litio)

Tranio
Is't possible, friend Litio, that Mistress Bianca doth fancy any other but Lucentio? I tell you, sir, she bears me fair in hand.

Hortensio
Sir, to satisfy you in what I have said, stand by and
5 mark the manner of his teaching.

> *They stand aside. Enter* Bianca *and* Lucentio (*as* Cambio)

Lucentio
Now, mistress, profit you in what you read?

Bianca
What, master, read you? First resolve me that.

Lucentio
I read that I profess, *The Art to Love*.

Bianca
And may you prove, sir, master of your art.

Lucentio
10 While you, sweet dear, prove mistress of my heart.

> *They move away.* Tranio *and* Hortensio *come forward*

11 *quick proceeders*: fast learners; 'proceed' is the technical term for a university scholar who moves to a higher degree — from 'bachelor' to 'master'.
12 *durst*: dare.
14 *despiteful*: cruel.
15 *wonderful*: incredible.

18 *scorn*: scorns; the singular verb agrees with 'I' in the preceding line.
20 *cullion*: peasant.

23 *entire affection to*: sincere love for.
24 *lightness*: unfaithfulness.

31 *fondly*: foolishly.
33 *though she would entreat*: even if she asked me to.
34 *beastly*: lasciviously; perhaps the lovers are kissing.
35 'I wish that everyone else would give up completely' — so that Bianca would have to marry her tutor; in his spite, Hortensio does not realize that this is exactly what Bianca wants.
36 *mine oath*: the vow he has just made.
37 *a wealthy widow*: This is the first time that this character has been mentioned; it may be that there has been some revision of the play, especially affecting the role and function of Hortensio.
39 *haggard*: Hortensio uses the same hawk imagery as Petruchio.
41 *Kindness*: affection, the readiness to love him.
43 *In resolution*: quite determined.

Hortensio
[*To* Tranio] Quick proceeders, marry! Now tell me, I
pray, you that durst swear that your mistress Bianca
loved none in the world so well as Lucentio—
  Tranio
O despiteful love, unconstant womankind!
15 I tell thee, Litio, this is wonderful.
  Hortensio
Mistake no more, I am not Litio,
Nor a musician as I seem to be,
But one that scorn to live in this disguise
For such a one as leaves a gentleman
20 And makes a god of such a cullion.
Know, sir, that I am called Hortensio.
  Tranio
Signor Hortensio, I have often heard
Of your entire affection to Bianca,
And since mine eyes are witness of her lightness,
25 I will with you, if you be so contented,
Forswear Bianca and her love for ever.
  Hortensio
See how they kiss and court! Signor Lucentio,
Here is my hand, and here I firmly vow
Never to woo her more, but do forswear her,
30 As one unworthy all the former favours
That I have fondly flattered her withal.
  Tranio
And here I take the like unfeigned oath
Never to marry with her though she would entreat.
Fie on her, see how beastly she doth court him!
  Hortensio
35 Would all the world but he had quite forsworn!
For me, that I may surely keep mine oath,
I will be married to a wealthy widow,
Ere three days pass, which hath as long loved me
As I have loved this proud disdainful haggard.
40 And so farewell, Signor Lucentio.
Kindness in women, not their beauteous looks,
Shall win my love, and so I take my leave,
In resolution as I swore before.
                             [*Exit*

    Lucentio *and* Bianca *come forward again*

45 *'longeth*: belongs.
   case: situation.
46 *ta'en you napping*: caught you by surprise.

51 *lusty*: merry.

58 *eleven-and-twenty long*: just the job, the right ones (compare *1, 2, 33 note*).
59 *charm*: put a spell on, silence.

61 *dog-weary*: tired out.
62 *ancient*: of the old style (i.e. trustworthy, honest; the adjective prepares for a double meaning in the noun).
   angel: messenger from heaven; *and* a gold coin stamped with the archangel Michael.
63 *serve the turn*: do for the job.
65 *marcantant*: merchant; presumably Biondello mispronounces the Italian *mercatante*.
   pedant: teacher; the pedant was one of the stock characters of the *commedia dell'arte*.
67 *countenance*: appearance.

Tranio
Mistress Bianca, bless you with such grace
45 As 'longeth to a lover's blessèd case!
Nay, I have ta'en you napping, gentle love,
And have forsworn you with Hortensio.

Bianca
Tranio, you jest — but have you both forsworn me?

Tranio
Mistress, we have.

Lucentio
50   Then we are rid of Litio.

Tranio
I'faith, he'll have a lusty widow now
That shall be wooed and wedded in a day.

Bianca
God give him joy!

Tranio   Ay, and he'll tame her.

Bianca
He says so Tranio?

Tranio
55 Faith, he is gone unto the taming-school.

Bianca
The taming-school? What, is there such a place?

Tranio
Ay, mistress, and Petruchio is the master
That teacheth tricks eleven-and-twenty long,
To tame a shrew and charm her chattering tongue.

Enter Biondello

Biondello
60 O master, master, I have watched so long
That I am dog-weary, but at last I spied
An ancient angel coming down the hill
Will serve the turn.

Tranio
What is he, Biondello?

Biondello
65 Master, a marcantant or a pedant,
I know not what, but formal in apparel,
In gait and countenance surely like a father.

Lucentio
And what of him, Tranio?

69 *trust my tale*: believe what I tell him.

70 *seem*: pretend to be.

75 *far on*: any farther.
at the farthest: as far as you go.

78 *if . . . life*: if I live long enough.

79 *What countryman*: Where do you come from?
Of Mantua: This Pedant is travelling an odd route; but Shakespeare is not interested in his itinerary: it is only important to establish that he is a complete stranger.

82 *goes hard*: sounds serious.

85 *stayed*: held up; Mantua is not a sea-port, but cities in northern Italy were linked by a network of canals.
the Duke: i.e. of Venice, who might also have been the ruler of Padua.

87 *published*: declared.

88-9 'If you were not such a stranger you would certainly have heard about it'; Tranio's sentence-structure suggests his excitement.

90 *worse . . . than*: even worse than that.

91 *bills . . . exchange*: notes which can be exchanged for cash.

92 *deliver*: exchange.

93 *do you courtesy*: do you a favour.

Tranio
If he be credulous and trust my tale,
70 I'll make him glad to seem Vincentio,
And give assurance to Baptista Minola
As if he were the right Vincentio.
Take in your love, and then let me alone.
                    [*Exeunt* Lucentio *and* Bianca

Enter a Pedant

Pedant
God save you, sir.
         Tranio   And you sir. You are welcome.
75 Travel you far on, or are you at the farthest?
         Pedant
Sir, at the farthest for a week or two,
But then up farther, and as far as Rome,
And so to Tripoli, if God lend me life.
         Tranio
What countryman, I pray?
         Pedant   Of Mantua.
         Tranio
80 Of Mantua, sir? Marry, God forbid!
And come to Padua, careless of your life?
         Pedant
My life, sir? How, I pray? For that goes hard.
         Tranio
'Tis death for anyone in Mantua
To come to Padua. Know you not the cause?
85 Your ships are stayed at Venice, and the Duke,
For private quarrel 'twixt your Duke and him,
Hath published and proclaimed it openly.
'Tis marvel, but that you are but newly come,
You might have heard it else proclaimed about.
         Pedant
90 Alas, sir, it is worse for me than so,
For I have bills for money by exchange
From Florence, and must here deliver them.
         Tranio
Well, sir, to do you courtesy,
This will I do, and this I will advise you:
95 First tell me, have you ever been at Pisa?

97 This seems to be a repetition of a
proverbial saying — compare *1*, 1, 10.
98 *one*: a certain.

Pedant
Ay, sir, in Pisa have I often been,
Pisa renowned for grave citizens.
Tranio
Among them know you one Vincentio?
Pedant
I know him not, but I have heard of him:
100 A merchant of incomparable wealth.
Tranio
He is my father, sir, and sooth to say,
In countenance somewhat doth resemble you.
Biondello
[*Aside*] As much as an apple doth an oyster, and all
one.

103 *apple . . . oyster*: A proverbial
comparison.
and all one: never mind about that.

104 *extremity*: danger.

Tranio
To save your life in this extremity,
105 This favour will I do you for his sake,
And think it not the worst of all your fortunes
That you are like to Sir Vincentio:
His name and credit shall you undertake,
And in my house you shall be friendly lodged.
110 Look that you take upon you as you should.
You understand me, sir. So shall you stay
Till you have done your business in the city.
If this be courtesy, sir, accept of it.
Pedant
O sir, I do, and will repute you ever
115 The patron of my life and liberty.
Tranio
Then go with me, to make the matter good.
This by the way, I let you understand:
My father is here looked for every day
To pass assurance of a dower in marriage
120 'Twixt me and one Baptista's daughter here.
In all these circumstances I'll instruct you.
Go with me to clothe you as becomes you.
[*Exeunt*

108 *credit*: position.
undertake: assume.
109 *friendly*: as a friend.
110 *Look that*: see to it that.
take upon you: do what is required of you.

113 *If . . . courtesy*: If you think I'm doing
you a kindness.
114 *repute*: consider.
115 *patron*: saviour.

116 *make the matter good*: put this plan into
action.
117 *by the way*: as we go along.
118 *looked for*: expected.
119 *pass assurance*: make a formal agreement.

121 *circumstances*: details.
122 *becomes you*: i.e. is appropriate for your
new identity (as Vincentio of Pisa).

Act 4   Scene 3

Once again the scene changes, and we are back in Petruchio's house where Katherina, very hungry and tired, is taunted by Grumio, who refuses to let her eat. Petruchio brings food, but again it is refused her. The new cap, made for Katherina by the Haberdasher, offends Petruchio's taste; so does the Tailor's new gown. The married couple are preparing to return to Padua, but when Katherina contradicts her husband once more, Petruchio abandons the expedition.

2 'The more I have to suffer, the worse his cruelty grows.'
5 *Upon entreaty*: as soon as they ask.
  present: immediate.
9 *meat*: food.

11 *spites*: hurts.
   wants: things I lack.
12 *under*: in the name of.
13 *As who*: like one who.
14 *present*: instant.
15 *repast*: nourishment.

17 *neat's foot*: ox-foot or calf's foot.

19 *choleric*: causing choler; Grumio obviously knows Petruchio's plan.
20 *tripe*: the stomach lining of a cow or sheep; served with onions, this is still a popular dish in the north of England.

22 *I cannot tell*: I'm not sure.

26 *let . . . rest*: forget the mustard.

Scene 3

Enter Katherina *and* Grumio

Grumio
No, no, forsooth, I dare not for my life.
Katherina
The more my wrong, the more his spite appears.
What, did he marry me to famish me?
Beggars that come unto my father's door
5 Upon entreaty have a present alms;
If not, elsewhere they meet with charity.
But I, who never knew how to entreat,
Nor never needed that I should entreat,
Am starved for meat, giddy for lack of sleep,
10 With oaths kept waking, and with brawling fed;
And that which spites me more than all these wants,
He does it under name of perfect love,
As who should say, if I should sleep or eat,
'Twere deadly sickness or else present death.
15 I prithee go and get me some repast,
I care not what, so it be wholesome food.
Grumio
What say you to a neat's foot?
Katherina
'Tis passing good, I prithee let me have it.
Grumio
I fear it is too choleric a meat.
20 How say you to a fat tripe finely broiled?
Katherina
I like it well. Good Grumio, fetch it me.
Grumio
I cannot tell, I fear 'tis choleric.
What say you to a piece of beef and mustard?
Katherina
A dish that I do love to feed upon.
Grumio
25 Ay, but the mustard is too hot a little.
Katherina
Why then the beef, and let the mustard rest.
Grumio
Nay then, I will not: you shall have the mustard,
Or else you get no beef of Grumio.

Katherina

Then both, or one, or anything thou wilt.

Grumio

30   Why then the mustard without the beef.

Katherina

Go, get thee gone, thou false deluding slave

She beats him

That feed'st me with the very name of meat.

Sorrow on thee and all the pack of you

That triumph thus upon my misery!

35   Go, get thee gone, I say.

Enter Petruchio *and* Hortensio *with meat*

Petruchio

How fares my Kate? What, sweeting, all amort?

Hortensio

Mistress, what cheer?

Katherina   Faith, as cold as can be.

Petruchio

Pluck up thy spirits, look cheerfully upon me.

Here, love, thou seest how diligent I am,

40   To dress thy meat myself, and bring it thee.

I am sure, sweet Kate, this kindness merits thanks.

What, not a word? Nay then, thou lov'st it not,

And all my pains is sorted to no proof.

Here, take away this dish.

Katherina   I pray you let it stand.

Petruchio

45   The poorest service is repaid with thanks,

And so shall mine before you touch the meat.

Katherina

I thank you, sir.

Hortensio

Signor Petruchio, fie, you are to blame.

Come, Mistress Kate, I'll bear you company.

Petruchio

50   [*Aside to* Hortensio] Eat it up all, Hortensio, if thou
     lovest me.

[*To* Katherina] Much good do it unto thy gentle
     heart!

Kate, eat apace. And now, my honey love,

Will we return unto thy father's house,

And revel it as bravely as the best,

32   *the very name*: the name and nothing else.

36   *sweeting*: sweetheart.
     amort: depressed.

37   *what cheer?*: how are you?
     cold: i.e. poor; Katherina refers to the
     hospitality — 'cheer' — of Petruchio's
     house.
38   *Pluck up*: lift up.

40   *dress*: prepare.

43   *pains*: trouble (treated as a singular noun).
     is . . . proof: has been in vain.
44   *let it stand*: leave it where it is;
     Katherina's completion of Petruchio's
     half-line shows the sharpness of her
     hunger.
46   *mine*: i.e. my service.

48   *blame*: blameworthy, at fault.
49   *bear you company*: join you (in the meal);
     Hortensio, like Grumio, seems to be a
     party to Petruchio's scheme.

52   *apace*: without hesitation (she is probably
     grabbing every morsel before Hortensio
     can eat it all up).
54   *revel it*: enjoy ourselves.
     bravely: finely dressed.

56 *ruffs and cuffs*: starched material — or perhaps lace — at neck and wrists; Petruchio begins to sound frivolous (especially in his rhymes), and this ought to be a warning to Katherina.
farthingales: hooped skirts, worn by women of the upper classes.

57 *bravery*: fine clothes.
58 *knavery*: nonsense.
59 *stays*: awaits.
60 *deck*: adorn.
    ruffling: decorated with ruffles.
63 *cap*: worn indoors by married women.
64 *porringer*: basin, especially for a child's food.
65 *A velvet dish*: nothing but a dish made of velvet.
    lewd and filthy: cheap and nasty.
66 *cockle*: cockle-shell.
67 *knack*: The word survives as part of 'knick-knack'; 'toy' and 'trick' have much the same meaning.
69 *doth fit the time*: is fashionable.
72 *in haste*: in a hurry, very soon.
73 *leave*: permission.
75 *endured me say*: let me speak.
78 *it*: i.e. her anger.
82 *custard-coffin*: pastry case for a baked custard.
83 *in that*: because.

55 With silken coats and caps, and golden rings,
With ruffs and cuffs, and farthingales, and things;
With scarfs and fans, and double change of bravery,
With amber bracelets, beads, and all this knavery.
What, hast thou dined? The tailor stays thy leisure,
60 To deck thy body with his ruffling treasure.

Enter Tailor

Come tailor, let us see these ornaments.
Lay forth the gown.

Enter Haberdasher

                    What news with you, sir?
Haberdasher
Here is the cap your worship did bespeak.
Petruchio
Why, this was moulded on a porringer;
65 A velvet dish! Fie, fie, 'tis lewd and filthy.
Why, 'tis a cockle or a walnut-shell,
A knack, a toy, a trick, a baby's cap.
Away with it; come, let me have a bigger.
Katherina
I'll have no bigger. This doth fit the time,
70 And gentlewomen wear such caps as these.
Petruchio
When you are gentle, you shall have one too,
And not till then.
Hortensio   That will not be in haste.
Katherina
Why sir, I trust I may have leave to speak,
And speak I will. I am no child, no babe;
75 Your betters have endured me say my mind,
And if you cannot, best you stop your ears.
My tongue will tell the anger of my heart,
Or else my heart concealing it will break,
And rather than it shall, I will be free
80 Even to the uttermost, as I please, in words.
Petruchio
Why, thou say'st true, it is a paltry cap,
A custard-coffin, a bauble, a silken pie:
I love thee well in that thou lik'st it not.

86 *Thy gown*: Perhaps Petruchio (wilfully) mishears Katherina's 'none' in the preceding line.
87 *masquing stuff*: fancy-dress costume.
88 *demi-cannon*: small cannon. See illustration.

91 *a censer in a barber's shop*: A censer is an incense-burner, but no-one seems to know why this should be found in a barber's shop. Perhaps it was some kind of air-freshener.
92 *a devil's name*: in the devil's name.
93 *like*: likely.
94 *bid*: bade, ordered.
95 *the time*: in the modern way.
96 *and did*: and so I did.
     be remembered: can remember.
97 *mar*: spoil.
98 *hop me . . . home*: hop off home.
     kennel: street gutter.
100 *make . . . it*: do what you can with it.
101 *better-fashioned*: more fashionable.
102 *quaint*: elegant.
103 *Belike*: it seems.
     puppet: doll (easily manipulated in puppet-shows); but Petruchio pretends that Katherina was speaking to the Tailor.

Katherina
Love me or love me not, I like the cap,
85 And it I will have, or I will have none.
     Petruchio
Thy gown? Why, ay. Come tailor, let us see't.
                    [*Exit* Haberdasher
O mercy, God, what masquing stuff is here?
What's this? A sleeve? 'Tis like a demi-cannon.
What, up and down carved like an apple tart?
90 Here's snip, and nip, and cut, and slish and slash,
Like to a censer in a barber's shop.
Why, what a devil's name, tailor, call'st thou this?
     Hortensio
[*Aside*] I see she's like to have neither cap nor gown.
     Tailor
You bid me make it orderly and well,
95 According to the fashion and the time.
     Petruchio
Marry, and did; but if you be remembered,
I did not bid you mar it to the time.
Go, hop me over every kennel home,
For you shall hop without my custom, sir;
100 I'll none of it. Hence, make your best of it.
     Katherina
I never saw a better-fashioned gown,
More quaint, more pleasing, nor more
     commendable.
Belike you mean to make a puppet of me.
     Petruchio
Why, true, he means to make a puppet of thee.
     Tailor
105 She says your worship means to make a puppet of
     her.
     Petruchio
O monstrous arrogance!
Thou liest, thou thread, thou thimble,
Thou yard, three-quarters, half-yard, quarter, nail,
Thou flea, thou nit, thou winter-cricket thou!
110 Braved in mine own house with a skein of thread?
Away, thou rag, thou quantity, thou remnant,
Or I shall so be-mete thee with thy yard
As thou shalt think on prating whilst thou liv'st.
I tell thee, I, that thou hast marred her gown.

108 *yard*: yardstick — a measuring rod for lengths of fabric; it was a common term of abuse for tailors (who were, by reputation, thin and effeminate). Petruchio's abusive eloquence extends far beyond the commonplace. The length of a yard is 92 centimetres.
nail: one-sixteenth of a yard (6 centimetres).

109 *nit*: the egg of a louse.
winter-cricket: insect that appears in the winter.

110 *Braved*: defied; there is a pun — which is developed in the next few lines — with the sense of 'smartly dressed'.

111 *quantity*: fragment.

112 *be-mete . . . yard*: measure you out with your own yardstick.

113 *think on*: remember.
while thou liv'st: for as long as you live.

118 *stuff*: material.

122 *faced*: trimmed with velvet or other fabric; *also* defied, dared.

127 *Ergo*: therefore; a term in logical debate.

128 *note of the fashion*: i.e. the pattern; Grumio takes up the sense of a muscial note.

130 *lies in's throat*: sticks in his throat — is an unspeakable lie.

131 *Imprimis*: first of all.
loose-bodied gown: loosely fitting gown; but Grumio pretends to interpret this as a dress for a loose-living woman.

133 *bottom*: bobbin.

136 *compassed*: flared, cut on the bias.

137 *confess*: admit.

138 *trunk sleeve*: large, wide sleeve.

Tailor

115 Your worship is deceived: the gown is made
Just as my master had direction;
Grumio gave order how it should be done.

Grumio

I gave him no order, I gave him the stuff.

Tailor

But how did you desire it should be made?

Grumio

120 Marry, sir, with needle and thread.

Tailor

But did you not request to have it cut?

Grumio

Thou hast faced many things?

Tailor

I have.

Grumio

Face not me. Thou hast braved many men; brave not
125 me: I will neither be faced nor braved. I say unto thee,
I bid thy master cut out the gown, but I did not bid
him cut it to pieces. Ergo thou liest.

Tailor

Why, here is the note of the fashion to testify.

Petruchio

Read it.

Grumio

130 The note lies in's throat if he say I said so.

Tailor

[*Reads*] '*Imprimis*, a loose-bodied gown.'

Grumio

Master, if ever I said 'loose-bodied gown', sew me in
the skirts of it and beat me to death with a bottom of
brown thread. I said 'a gown'.

Petruchio

135 [*To the* Tailor] Proceed.

Tailor

'With a small compassed cape.'

Grumio

I confess the cape.

Tailor

'With a trunk sleeve.'

140 *curiously*: carefully, elaborately.

142 *Error i'th'bill*: mistaken charge; the phrase is legal jargon — a criminal charge would fail if there were any error in the formal indictment.

144 *prove upon*: prove against; Grumio is preparing for a fight.

146 *an*: if only.
in place where: in the right place.

148 *for thee*: ready to fight you.
straight: right now.
bill: the order-note; *and* a weapon used by watchmen.

149 *mete-yard*: measuring-stick.

150 *odds*: chance (if he is armed only with the piece of paper).

154–5 *take . . . use*: take it away and let your master do the best he can with it; but Grumio misunderstands.

156 *conceit*: meaning.

157 *think for*: imagine.

158 *use*: (sexual) purposes.

159 Petruchio ensures that the bewildered Tailor shall not suffer.

Grumio
I confess two sleeves.

Tailor
'The sleeves curiously cut.'

Petruchio
Ay, there's the villainy.

Grumio
Error i'th' bill, sir, error i'th' bill! I commanded the sleeves should be cut out, and sewed up again, and that I'll prove upon thee, though thy little finger be armed in a thimble.

Tailor
This is true that I say; an I had thee in place where, thou shouldst know it.

Grumio
I am for thee straight. Take thou the bill, give me thy mete-yard, and spare not me.

Hortensio
God-a-mercy, Grumio, then he shall have no odds.

Petruchio
[*To the* Tailor] Well sir, in brief, the gown is not for me.

Grumio
You are i' the right, sir, 'tis for my mistress.

Petruchio
Go, take it up unto thy master's use.

Grumio
Villain, not for thy life! Take up my mistress' gown for thy master's use?

Petruchio
Why sir, what's your conceit in that?

Grumio
O sir, the conceit is deeper than you think for. Take up my mistress' gown to his master's use? O fie, fie, fie!

Petruchio
[*Aside*] Hortensio, say thou wilt see the tailor paid.
[*To the* Tailor] Go take it hence, be gone, and say no more.

Hortensio
[*Aside to the* Tailor] Tailor, I'll pay thee for thy gown tomorrow;

162 *no unkindness of*: no offence at.

Take no unkindness of his hasty words.
Away, I say, commend me to thy master.
[*Exit* Tailor

Petruchio
Well, come my Kate, we will unto your father's

165 *honest mean habiliments*: respectable everyday clothes.
166 *proud*: rich (because they have not wasted money).
167 This sounds like a topic for the lecture that follows.
169 *peereth*: can be seen through.
170 *jay*: a loud-voiced, chattering bird. *lark*: a plain brown bird, valued for its singing.
173 *painted*: patterned.

165 Even in these honest mean habiliments.
Our purses shall be proud, our garments poor,
For 'tis the mind that makes the body rich;
And as the sun breaks through the darkest clouds,
So honour peereth in the meanest habit.
170 What, is the jay more precious than the lark
Because his feathers are more beautiful?
Or is the adder better than the eel
Because his painted skin contents the eye?
O no, good Kate; neither art thou the worse

175 *furniture*: equipment. *mean array*: poor clothes.
176 *account'st*: consider. *lay it on me*: blame me.
177 *frolic*: be merry.
183 *by dinner-time*: in time for the main meal, usually served before noon.
185 *supper-time*: time for the evening meal, served before 6 p.m.

175 For this poor furniture and mean array.
If thou account'st it shame, lay it on me,
And therefore frolic: we will hence forthwith
To feast and sport us at thy father's house.
[*To* Grumio] Go call my men, and let us straight to him,
180 And bring our horses unto Long-lane end;
There will we mount, and thither walk on foot.
Let's see, I think 'tis now some seven o'clock,
And well we may come there by dinner-time.

Katherina
I dare assure you, sir, 'tis almost two,
185 And 'twill be supper-time ere you come there.

Petruchio
It shall be seven ere I go to horse.

187 *Look what*: whatever.
188 *still*: always. *crossing*: contradicting. *let't*: leave it.
189 *ere I do*: before I go at all.
190 *what o'clock*: whatever time.

Look what I speak, or do, or think to do,
You are still crossing it. Sirs, let't alone,
I will not go today; and ere I do,
190 It shall be what o'clock I say it is.

Hortensio
[*Aside*] Why, so this gallant will command the sun.
[*Exeunt*

Act 4 Scene 4

Once more in Padua, we find that Tranio (still disguised as Lucentio) is about to introduce the traveller (whom he met in Scene 3) to Baptista. Arrangements are made for Bianca's marriage, but because Baptista prefers not to discuss the financial details in his own house, Tranio leads them away, leaving Biondello to give directions to the real Lucentio, who is to elope with Bianca and find St Luke's church, where a priest waits to marry them.

os.d. *booted*: The Pedant still wears his travelling boots — a reminder for the audience that he is not the real Vincentio.

1 *please it you*: do you wish me to knock: Tranio speaks with the courtesy of a son.

2 *what else*: of course; the Pedant is entering into his role as Vincentio — his next three lines seem to be solely for the purpose of forming his new character.
   but I be: unless I am.

5 *Pegasus*: the name of an inn, whose sign was the flying horse of Greek mythology.

6 *'Tis well*: Tranio approves the Pedant's acting.
   hold . . . case: keep it up whatever you do.

7 *austerity*: gravity.
   'longeth: belongs to, is proper for.

8 *warrant*: promise.

9 *schooled*: told what to do.

10 *Fear . . . him*: don't worry about him.

11 *throughly*: perfectly.
    advise: warn.

12 *right*: real.

16 *looked for*: expected.

17 *tall fellow*: good chap.
    hold . . . drink: take that and buy yourself a drink.

Scene 4

Enter Tranio (*as* Lucentio), *and the*
Pedant, *booted but dressed like* Vincentio

Tranio
Sir, this is the house; please it you that I call?
        Pedant
Ay, what else? And but I be deceived
Signor Baptista may remember me
Near twenty years ago in Genoa,
5 Where we were lodgers at the Pegasus.
        Tranio
'Tis well, and hold your own in any case
With such austerity as 'longeth to a father.

Enter Biondello

        Pedant
I warrant you. But sir, here comes your boy.
'Twere good he were schooled.
        Tranio
10 Fear you not him. — Sirrah Biondello,
Now do your duty throughly, I advise you.
Imagine 'twere the right Vincentio.
        Biondello
Tut, fear not me.
        Tranio
But hast thou done thy errand to Baptista?
        Biondello
15 I told him that your father was at Venice,
And that you looked for him this day in Padua.
        Tranio
Thou'rt a tall fellow, hold thee that to drink.
        He gives Biondello *money*
[*To the* Pedant] Here comes Baptista. Set your
countenance, sir.

Enter Baptista, *and* Lucentio (*as* Cambio).
The Pedant *stands bare-headed*

— Signor Baptista, you are happily met.
20 — Sir, this is the gentleman I told you of.
I pray you stand good father to me now,
Give me Bianca for my patrimony.

18   *Set your countenance*: i.e. put your act on.
18s.d.   *bare-headed*: i.e. in respect to Baptista.
21   *stand good father*: show yourself to be a good father.
22   *patrimony*: inheritance.
23   *Soft*: steady.
24   *gather in*: collect.
25   *weighty cause*: important matter.
27   *for*: because of.
29   *stay*: delay.
31   *have him matched*: let him get married.
     like: approve.
34   *one consent*: in full agreement; the Pedant seems to be struggling a little with his formal language.
     bestowed: given in marriage.
35   *curious I cannot be*: I don't want to make difficulties.
38   *shortness*: brevity (in speaking).
41   *dissemble*: pretend.
43   *deal with him*: treat.
44   *pass*: allow.
46   *with consent*: with my blessing.
48   *be affied*: may be formally betrothed (a ceremony before witnesses that was socially almost as binding as a wedding in church — see *Act 2 Scene 1 line 321 note*).
     assurance: legal guarantees.
51   *Pitchers have ears*: A proverbial saying that means 'everybody is listening' (*pitchers* are water-jugs, whose handles were called *ears*).

52   *hearkening still*: always listening in.
53   *happily*: perhaps.
55   *lie*: lodge.
56   *pass*: transact.
57   *your servant here*: Lucentio (disguised as Cambio); as he indicates the 'servant', Tranio must give him a nod or wink (see line 74).
58   *my boy*: i.e. Biondello.
     scrivener: legal writer.
     presently: immediately.
59   *slender warning*: short notice.
60   'There probably won't be much to eat.'

Pedant
Soft, son! — Sir, by your leave: having come to Padua
To gather in some debts, my son Lucentio
25 Made me acquainted with a weighty cause
Of love between your daughter and himself;
And for the good report I hear of you,
And for the love he beareth to your daughter,
And she to him, to stay him not too long,
30 I am content, in a good father's care,
To have him matched; and, if you please to like
No worse than I, upon some agreement
Me shall you find ready and willing
With one consent to have her so bestowed;
35 For curious I cannot be with you,
Signor Baptista, of whom I hear so well.

Baptista
Sir, pardon me in what I have to say.
Your plainness and your shortness please me well.
Right true it is your son Lucentio here
40 Doth love my daughter, and she loveth him,
Or both dissemble deeply their affections,
And therefore if you say no more than this,
That like a father you will deal with him,
And pass my daughter a sufficient dower,
45 That match is made, and all is done;
Your son shall have my daughter with consent.

Tranio
I thank you, sir. Where then do you know best
We be affied and such assurance ta'en
As shall with either part's agreement stand?

Baptista
50 Not in my house, Lucentio, for you know
Pitchers have ears, and I have many servants.
Besides, old Gremio is hearkening still,
And happily we might be interrupted.

Tranio
Then at my lodging, an it like you.
55 There doth my father lie; and there this night
We'll pass the business privately and well.
Send for your daughter by your servant here;
My boy shall fetch the scrivener presently.
The worst is this, that at so slender warning
60 You are like to have a thin and slender pittance.

62 *make her*: get herself.
63 *if you will*: if you want to.

67 *Dally not*: don't waste time.
  get thee gone: Biondello cannot exit here,
  since he is required to speak at line 72,
  explaining at line 77 that he has been 'left
  . . . here behind'.
69 *One mess*: a single dish.
  your cheer: all the hospitality you will
  receive.
70 *better it in Pisa*: i.e. improve things when
  we get home.

79 *moralize them*: interpret them.

80 *safe*: safely out of the way.

Baptista
It likes me well. Cambio, hie you home,
And bid Bianca make her ready straight;
And, if you will, tell what hath happened:
Lucentio's father is arrived in Padua,
65 And how she's like to be Lucentio's wife.
  Biondello
I pray the gods she may, with all my heart.
                              [*Exit* Lucentio
  Tranio
Dally not with the gods, but get thee gone.
— Signor Baptista, shall I lead the way?
Welcome! One mess is like to be your cheer.
70 Come sir, we will better it in Pisa.
  Baptista
I follow you.
                    [*Exeunt all except* Biondello

        Enter Lucentio (*as* Cambio)

  Biondello
Cambio.
  Lucentio
What say'st thou, Biondello?
  Biondello
You saw my master wink and laugh upon you?
  Lucentio
75 Biondello, what of that?
  Biondello
Faith, nothing; but h'as left me here behind
to expound the meaning or moral of his signs and
tokens.
  Lucentio
I pray thee moralize them.
  Biondello
80 Then thus: Baptista is safe talking with the deceiving
father of a deceitful son.
  Lucentio
And what of him?
  Biondello
His daughter is to be brought by you to the supper.
  Lucentio
And then?

Biondello

85 The old priest at Saint Luke's church is at your
command at all hours.

Lucentio

And what of all this?

Biondello

I cannot tell, except they are busied about a counterfeit
assurance. Take you assurance of her, *cum privilegio ad*
90 *impremendum solum*. To th' church take the priest,
clerk, and some sufficient honest witnesses.
    If this be not that you look for, I have no more to
    say,
    But bid Bianca farewell for ever and a day.

[*Going*

Lucentio

Hear'st thou, Biondello—

Biondello

95 I cannot tarry. I knew a wench married in an afternoon
as she went to the garden for parsley to stuff a rabbit;
and so may you, sir; and so adieu, sir. My master hath
appointed me to go to Saint Luke's to bid the priest be
ready to come against you come with your appendix.

[*Exit*

Lucentio

100 I may and will, if she be so contented.
    She will be pleased, then wherefore should I doubt?
    Hap what hap may, I'll roundly go about her;
    It shall go hard if Cambio go without her.

[*Exit*

89–90 Biondello urges Lucentio to get full
possession of Bianca by marrying her; the
Latin phrase was used by Elizabethan
printers to indicate their licence to print a
book, interpreting the Latin as meaning
'with the sole right to print'.
91 *sufficient*: competent.
92 *look for*: are hoping for.

99 *against*: for when.
    appendix: appendage — i.e. wife;
    Biondello's word continues the printing-
    house imagery.

102 *Hap what hap may*: come what may — a
    proverbial expression.

Act 4   Scene 5

Petruchio and Katherina, accompanied by
Hortensio, have started their journey to
Baptista's house; they argue about the time of
day — and we see that Katherina is now very
much reformed. Encountering an old man on
the road, Petruchio makes further trial of his
wife's obedience; and he is satisfied. The old
man proves to be Lucentio's father — the real
Vincentio — and they travel on together to
Padua.

1 *a*: in.

Scene 5

Enter Petruchio, Katherina, *and*
Hortensio

Petruchio

Come on, a God's name, once more toward our
    father's.
Good Lord, how bright and goodly shines the moon!

Katherina

The moon? The sun; it is not moonlight now.

Petruchio

I say it is the moon that shines so bright.

7 *list*: like.
8 *Or e'er*: before.
9 The party is obviously walking to 'Long-
   lane end' — where Petruchio arranged to
   meet the horses in *4, 3, 180–1*.
10 *crossed*: contradicted.

14 *rush-candle*: cheap candle made by dipping
   the pith of a rush into tallow.

20 *even as your mind*: whenever you want it
   to (Katherina also implies that Petruchio
   changes his mind with the moon — that
   he is lunatic).

23 *go thy ways*: carry on (an exclamation of
   praise).

25 *unluckily*: unnaturally.
   against the bias: In the game of bowls, one
   side of the bowl is weighted — with a
   bias — to give a natural curving path.

27 *where away*: where are you going.

29 *fresher*: healthier.

30 *war*: contest; the imagery is an
   Elizabethan commonplace.

Katherina

5   I know it is the sun that shines so bright.

Petruchio

Now by my mother's son, and that's myself,
It shall be moon, or star, or what I list,
Or e'er I journey to your father's house.
[*To* Hortensio] Go on and fetch our horses back
   again.

10 — Evermore crossed and crossed, nothing but
   crossed!

Hortensio

[*To* Katherina] Say as he says, or we shall never go.

Katherina

Forward, I pray, since we have come so far,
And be it moon, or sun, or what you please;
And if you please to call it a rush-candle,

15 Henceforth I vow it shall be so for me.

Petruchio

I say it is the moon.

Katherina

                    I know it is the moon.

Petruchio

Nay, then you lie. It is the blessèd sun.

Katherina

Then, God be blessed, it is the blessèd sun,
But sun it is not, when you say it is not,

20 And the moon changes even as your mind:
What you will have it named, even that it is,
And so it shall be so for Katherine.

Hortensio

Petruchio, go thy ways, the field is won.

Petruchio

Well, forward, forward, thus the bowl should run,

25 And not unluckily against the bias.
But soft, company is coming here.

Enter Vincentio

[*To* Vincentio] Good morrow, gentle mistress, where
   away?
—Tell me, sweet Kate, and tell me truly too.
Hast thou beheld a fresher gentlewoman?

30 Such war of white and red within her cheeks!
What stars do spangle heaven with such beauty

32 *become*: suit, look lovely in.

35 *A*: he.
   make the woman: make him play a
   woman's part.

39 *favourable stars*: a happy fate.

46 *green*: in colour; *also* young.
47 *reverend*: to be revered.

54 *My name is called*: Vincentio uses the old-
   fashioned idiom; compare 2, 1, 67.
55 *bound I am*: I am going.

60 *entitle*: address you with the title.
62 *by this*: by this time; Petruchio should not
   know this — in fact it has not yet
   happened in the play. It seems that the
   two actions — the Katherina/Petruchio
   plot and the Bianca/Lucentio romance —
   operate in different time zones.

63 *esteem*: reputation.

As those two eyes become that heavenly face?
—Fair lovely maid, once more good day to thee.
—Sweet Kate, embrace her for her beauty's sake.
> **Hortensio**
35 [*Aside*] A will make the man mad, to make the
woman of him.
> **Katherina**
Young budding virgin, fair, and fresh, and sweet,
Whither away, or where is thy abode?
Happy the parents of so fair a child;
Happier the man whom favourable stars
40 Allots thee for his lovely bedfellow.
> **Petruchio**
Why, how now, Kate, I hope thou art not mad:
This is a man, old, wrinkled, faded, withered,
And not a maiden, as thou say'st he is.
> **Katherina**
Pardon, old father, my mistaking eyes
45 That have been so bedazzled with the sun
That everything I look on seemeth green.
Now I perceive thou art a reverend father;
Pardon, I pray thee, for my mad mistaking.
> **Petruchio**
Do, good old grandsire, and withal make known
50 Which way thou travellest; if along with us,
We shall be joyful of thy company.
> **Vincentio**
Fair sir, and you my merry mistress,
That with your strange encounter much amazed me,
My name is called Vincentio, my dwelling Pisa,
55 And bound I am to Padua, there to visit
A son of mine, which long I have not seen.
> **Petruchio**
What is his name?
> **Vincentio**
> > Lucentio, gentle sir.
> **Petruchio**
Happily met, the happier for thy son.
And now by law, as well as reverend age,
60 I may entitle thee my loving father.
The sister to my wife, this gentlewoman,
Thy son by this hath married. Wonder not,
Nor be not grieved: she is of good esteem,

Her dowry wealthy, and of worthy birth;
65 Beside, so qualified as may beseem
The spouse of any noble gentleman.
Let me embrace with old Vincentio,
And wander we to see thy honest son,
Who will of thy arrival be full joyous.

Vincentio
70 But is this true, or is it else your pleasure,
Like pleasant travellers, to break a jest
Upon the company you overtake?

Hortensio
I do assure thee, father, so it is.

Petruchio
Come, go along and see the truth hereof,
75 For our first merriment hath made thee jealous.

[*Exeunt all but* Hortensio

Hortensio
Well, Petruchio, this has put me in heart.
Have to my widow, and if she be froward,
Then hast thou taught Hortensio to be untoward.

[*Exit*

65 *so qualified*: with such good qualities.
beseem: be appropriate for.

68 *wander we*: let's travel on.
69 *of*: at.

71 *pleasant*: light-hearted.
break a jest: play a trick.

75 *merriment*: joking.
jealous: suspicious.

76 *put me in heart*: given me encouragement.
77 *Have to*: forward to, now for.
froward: obstinate.
78 *untoward*: intractable — equally obstinate.

Act 5

Act 5 Scene 1

This is a scene of great activity, as the different strands of the play are brought together: Bianca and Lucentio go off to church; Petruchio brings Katherina to Padua; the disguised Vincentio meets the real one, and Biondello gets a beating. Tranio attempts to continue the deception of Baptista, until the married Lucentio returns and all is made plain. All the characters leave to share in the wedding-feast; but before they go, Katherina kisses her husband.

os.d. *Gremio*: In *4,4,52* Baptista complained that 'old Gremio is hearkening still', and now the Folio text indicates that the suspicious old man should be 'out before' to listen to what is going on.

4 *see . . . back*: get you to the church.

6 Gremio does not recognize Lucentio, who is no longer disguised as the tutor.

8 *My father's*: i.e. Baptista's house.
bears more toward: is more in the direction of.
9 *must I*: must I go.
10 *You . . . drink*: you must have a drink.

11 *I think I shall*: I'm sure I shall be able to.
12 *some cheer is toward*: there will be some refreshments available; Vincentio speaks with suitable formal courtesy.
13 *within*: inside there; Gremio is interfering.

Scene 1

Gremio *enters alone and stands aside. Then enter* Biondello, Lucentio *(no longer in disguise), and* Bianca

Biondello
Softly and swiftly, sir, for the priest is ready.
Lucentio
I fly, Biondello; but they may chance to need thee at home, therefore leave us.
[*Exeunt* Lucentio *and* Bianca
Biondello
Nay, faith, I'll see the church a' your back, and then
5 come back to my master's as soon as I can.
[*Exit
Gremio
I marvel Cambio comes not all this while.

Enter Petruchio, Katherina, Vincentio, *and* Grumio, *with* attendants

Petruchio
Sir, here's the door, this is Lucentio's house.
My father's bears more toward the market-place;
Thither must I, and here I leave you, sir.
Vincentio
10 You shall not choose but drink before you go.
I think I shall command your welcome here,
And by all likelihood some cheer is toward.

He knocks

Gremio
They're busy within, you were best knock louder.

Pedant *looks out of the window*

14   *as he*: as if he.

22-3   *leave frivolous circumstances*: forget about minor details.

26   *from Mantua*: The Folio text has 'from Padua', which is clearly wrong; perhaps the Pedant betrays himself by giving his own address.

31   *flat*: downright.

32   *a means*: he means.
       cozen: cheat.
33   *under my countenance*: by impersonating me.

35   *good shipping*: all success.
36-7   *brought to nothing*: utterly ruined.

38   *crack-hemp*: A term of abuse, referring to one fit only for hanging, who would stretch the hempen rope on the gallows.
39   *choose*: i.e. whether to come or go (= don't order me around).

Pedant
What's he that knocks as he would beat down the gate?
Vincentio
15   Is Signor Lucentio within, sir?
Pedant
He's within, sir, but not to be spoken withal.
Vincentio
What if a man bring him a hundred pound or two to make merry withal?
Pedant
Keep your hundred pounds to yourself, he shall need
20   none so long as I live.
Petruchio
[*To* Vincentio] Nay, I told you your son was well beloved in Padua. — Do you hear, sir? To leave frivolous circumstances, I pray you tell Signor Lucentio that his father is come from Pisa and is here
25   at the door to speak with him.
Pedant
Thou liest. His father is come from Mantua and here looking out at the window.
Vincentio
Art thou his father?
Pedant
Ay sir, so his mother says, if I may believe her.
Petruchio
30   [*To* Vincentio] Why how now, gentleman! Why, this is flat knavery, to take upon you another man's name.
Pedant
Lay hands on the villain: I believe a means to cozen somebody in this city under my countenance.

Enter Biondello

Biondello
[*Aside*] I have seen them in the church together. God
35   send 'em good shipping! But who is here? Mine old master Vincentio? Now we are undone and brought to nothing.
Vincentio
Come hither, crack-hemp.
Biondello
I hope I may choose, sir.

Vincentio

40 Come hither, you rogue. What, have you forgot
me?

Biondello

Forgot you? No, sir, I could not forget you, for I never
saw you before in all my life.

Vincentio

What, you notorious villain, didst thou never see thy
45 master's father, Vincentio?

Biondello

What, my old worshipful old master? Yes, marry, sir,
see where he looks out of the window.

Vincentio

Is't so, indeed?

He beats Biondello

Biondello

Help, help, help! Here's a madman will murder me.

[*Exit*

Pedant

50 Help, son! Help, Signor Baptista!

[*He leaves the window*

Petruchio

Prithee, Kate, let's stand aside and see the end of
this controversy.

Enter Pedant *from the house, with*
Servants; Baptista, *and* Tranio (*as*
Lucentio)

Tranio

Sir, what are you that offer to beat my servant?

Vincentio

What am I sir? Nay, what are you, sir? O immortal
55 gods! O fine villain! A silken doublet, a velvet hose, a
scarlet cloak, and a copatain hat! O, I am undone, I am
undone: while I play the good husband at home, my
son and my servant spend all at the university.

Tranio

How now, what's the matter?

Baptista

60 What, is the man lunatic?

44   *notorious*: exceptional.

53   *offer*: presume.
55   *a velvet hose*: pair of velvet breeches.
56   *a copatain hat*: See illustration; such hats
were not to be worn by servants.

57   *play . . . husband*: manage my money
carefully.

61 *sober ancient*: respectable old.
    by your habit: to judge by your clothes.
63 *what 'cerns it you*: what does it concern
    you.
64 *maintain*: afford.

66 *Bergamo*: A small town in northern Italy,
    Bergamo was not a sea-port and has never
    been known for sail-making; it is famous
    as the traditional home of Harlequin, the
    intriguing clown of the *commedia dell'arte*,
    and for its rough dialect.

81 *forthcoming*: brought to trial.

86 *cony-catched*: cheated, made a fool of.

Tranio
Sir, you seem a sober ancient gentleman by your habit,
but your words show you a madman. Why, sir, what
'cerns it you if I wear pearl and gold? I thank my good
father, I am able to maintain it.
Vincentio
65 Thy father? O villain, he is a sail-maker in
Bergamo.
Baptista
You mistake, sir, you mistake, sir. Pray, what do you
think is his name?
Vincentio
His name? As if I knew not his name! I have brought
70 him up ever since he was three years old, and his name
is Tranio.
Pedant
Away, away, mad ass, his name is Lucentio, and he is
mine only son, and heir to the lands of me, Signor
Vincentio.
Vincentio
75 Lucentio? O, he hath murdered his master! Lay hold
on him, I charge you, in the Duke's name. O my son,
my son! Tell me, thou villain, where is my son
Lucentio?
Tranio
Call forth an officer.

Enter an Officer

80 Carry this mad knave to the jail. Father Baptista, I
charge you see that he be forthcoming.
Vincentio
Carry me to the jail?
Gremio
Stay, officer, he shall not go to prison.
Baptista
Talk not, Signor Gremio; I say he shall go to
85 prison.
Gremio
Take heed, Signor Baptista, lest you be cony-catched
in this business. I dare swear this is the right
Vincentio.
Pedant
Swear if thou dar'st.

90 *I dare not*: Gremio's courage deserts him.

Gremio
90 Nay, I dare not swear it.
Tranio
Then thou wert best say that I am not Lucentio.
Gremio
Yes, I know thee to be Signor Lucentio.
Baptista

93 *dotard*: imbecile.

Away with the dotard, to the jail with him!

Enter Biondello, Lucentio, *and* Bianca

94 *haled*: dragged about.
  abused: misused.

Vincentio
Thus strangers may be haled and abused. O monstrous
95 villain!
Biondello
O, we are spoiled, and yonder he is! Deny him,
forswear him, or else we are all undone.
   [*Exeunt* Biondello, Tranio, *and* Pedant, *as fast as may be*
Lucentio
[*Kneeling*] Pardon, sweet father.
Vincentio   Lives my sweet son?
Bianca
Pardon, dear father.
Baptista   How hast thou offended?
100 Where is Lucentio?
Lucentio   Here's Lucentio,
Right son to the right Vincentio,
That have by marriage made thy daughter mine,
While counterfeit supposes bleared thine eyne.

103 *supposes*: suppositions; in this word,
Shakespeare alludes to the narrative from
which he took the story of Bianca and
Lucentio, George Gascoigne's *Supposes*
(which was a translation of Ariosto's *I
Suppositi*)
  bleared thine eyne: dimmed your eyes.
104 *packing*: conspiracy.
  with a witness: and no mistake.
106 *faced and braved*: defied; compare
4,3,122–5.

Gremio
Here's packing, with a witness, to deceive us all!
Vincentio
105 Where is that damned villain, Tranio,
That faced and braved me in this matter so?
Baptista
Why, tell me, is not this my Cambio.
Bianca
Cambio is changed into Lucentio.
Lucentio
Love wrought these miracles. Bianca's love

110 *state*: rank.
111 *bear my countenance*: impersonate me.
112 *happily*: luckily.

110 Made me exchange my state with Tranio,
While he did bear my countenance in the town,
And happily I have arrived at the last

Unto the wished haven of my bliss.
What Tranio did, myself enforced him to;
115 Then pardon him, sweet father, for my sake.
Vincentio
I'll slit the villain's nose that would have sent me to
the jail.
Baptista
[*To* Lucentio] But do you hear, sir, have you
married my daughter without asking my good will?
Vincentio
120 Fear not, Baptista, we will content you, go to. But I
will in, to be revenged for this villainy.
[*Exit*
Baptista
And I to sound the depth of this knavery.
[*Exit with* Officer
Lucentio
Look not pale, Bianca, thy father will not frown.
[*Exeunt* Lucentio *and* Bianca
Gremio
My cake is dough, but I'll in among the rest,
125 Out of hope of all but my share of the feast.
[*Exit*
Katherina
Husband, let's follow, to see the end of this ado.
Petruchio
First kiss me, Kate, and we will.
Katherina
What, in the midst of the street?
Petruchio
What, art thou ashamed of me?
Katherina
130 No sir, God forbid, but ashamed to kiss.
Petruchio
Why then, let's home again [*To* Grumio] Come,
sirrah, let's away.
Katherina
Nay, I will give thee a kiss. Now pray thee, love, stay.
Petruchio
Is not this well? Come, my sweet Kate.
135 Better once than never, for never too late.
[*Exeunt*

118 *do you hear*: look here.

120 *go to*: stop worrying.
121 *in*: go in (presumably he intends to beat Tranio).

122 *sound the depth*: learn the full extent.

124 *My cake is dough*: I've certainly lost; compare *1*,1,108.
125 *Out of hope of all*: not hoping for anything.

127 *kiss me, Kate*: compare *2*,1,326.

135 Petruchio combines two proverbs, 'Better late than never' and 'It is never too late to mend'.

Act 5   Scene 2

The three married couples — Katherina and Petruchio, Bianca and Lucentio, and Hortensio with his Widow — are sharing a wedding banquet. The women argue, whilst the men enjoy the fun. The women go into another room, and the husbands decide to place bets on their wives' obedience. Petruchio is the winner, and Katherina teaches a lesson to Bianca and the Widow.

0s.d *banquet*: final course of sweets, fruit, and wine that followed the main meal; dessert.
1 *though long*: only after a long time.
jarring: discordant.
agree: are in harmony.
3 *scapes*: escapes.
overblown: blown over, passed away.
5 *kindness*: courtesy; *and* kinship.
8 *with the best*: on the best food.
welcome to my house: The full wedding-feast would have been eaten in Baptista's house.
9 *close . . . up*: finish off our meal.
10 *great good cheer*: splendid reception.

13 *Padua affords this kindness*: this is normal hospitality in Padua; by calling Petruchio 'son', Baptista implies that he is now part of the society in Padua.

15 *would*: wish.

16 *for my life*: upon my life.
fears: is frightened of; but the Widow misunderstands.
17 'Believe me, I'm not scared.'

18 *sensible*: sensitive; *and* intelligent.
sense: meaning.

20 The Widow answers Petruchio with a trite proverb, meaning that people always judge everything from their own position — i.e. because Petruchio is afraid of *his* wife, he assumes that Hortensio must feel the same.
21 *Roundly*: smartly.
22 *conceive by*: understand; Petruchio wilfully misunderstands.
23 *likes Hortensio*: does Hortensio like.

Scene 2

Enter Baptista, Vincentio, Gremio, *the* Pedant, Lucentio *with* Bianca, Hortensio *with the* Widow, Tranio, Biondello, *and* Grumio, *followed by* Petruchio *and* Katherina. *The* Servingmen *bring in a banquet*

Lucentio
At last, though long, our jarring notes agree,
And time it is when raging war is done
To smile at scapes and perils overblown.
My fair Bianca, bid my father welcome,
5   While I with selfsame kindness welcome thine.
Brother Petruchio, sister Katherina,
And thou, Hortensio, with thy loving widow,
Feast with the best, and welcome to my house.
My banquet is to close our stomachs up
10 After our great good cheer. Pray you sit down,
For now we sit to chat as well as eat.
Petruchio
Nothing but sit and sit, and eat and eat!
Baptista
Padua affords this kindness, son Petruchio.
Petruchio
Padua affords nothing but what is kind.
Hortensio
15 For both our sakes I would that word were true.
Petruchio
Now, for my life, Hortensio fears his widow.
Widow
Then never trust me if I be afeard.
Petruchio
You are very sensible, and yet you miss my sense:
I mean Hortensio is afeard of you.
Widow
20 He that is giddy thinks the world turns round.
Petruchio
Roundly replied.
Katherina
                    Mistress, how mean you that?
Widow
Thus I conceive by him.

24 *conceives her tale*: understands the
meaning.

25 *mended*: saved.

28 *shrew*: The modern equivalent insult
would be 'bitch'.
29 *his*: his own — i.e. Petruchio's.

31 *mean*: cheap and nasty; but Katherina
next uses the adjective in the sense of
'moderate', 'respectable' — and even
'chaste' (since it was popularly thought
that widows who remarried must be
lustful).

33 *To her*: The husbands urge on their wives
as though they were at a prize-fight —
and then lay bets on the outcome.

35 *put her down*: beat the Widow.

36 *my office*: my job (as a husband).

37 *ha' to thee*: here's to you.

39 *butt together*: bang their heads together
(like young cattle).
40 *Head and butt*: are you talking of butting
heads.
hasty-witted body: quick-thinking person.
41 *horn*: Bianca alludes to the horn said to
grow on a cuckold's head; she has no
particular reason to insult Gremio like
this, but Shakespeare is preparing her
character for a change in function.
42 *awakened you*: Vincentio notes Bianca's
sudden arousal.

Petruchio
Conceives by me! How likes Hortensio that?
    Hortensio
My widow says, thus she conceives her tale.
    Petruchio
25 Very well mended. Kiss him for that, good widow.
    Katherina
'He that is giddy thinks the world turns round'—
I pray you tell me what you meant by that.
    Widow
Your husband, being troubled with a shrew,
Measures my husband's sorrow by his woe.
30 And now you know my meaning.
    Katherina
A very mean meaning.
    Widow
                                Right, I mean you.
    Katherina
And I am mean, indeed, respecting you.
    Petruchio
To her, Kate!
    Hortensio
To her widow!
    Petruchio
35 A hundred marks, my Kate does put her down.
    Hortensio
That's my office.
    Petruchio
Spoke like an officer — ha' to thee, lad.
                    He drinks to Hortensio.
    Baptista
How likes Gremio these quick-witted folks?
    Gremio
Believe me, sir, they butt together well.
    Bianca
40 Head and butt? An hasty-witted body
Would say your head and butt were head and horn.
    Vincentio
Ay, mistress bride, hath that awakened you?
    Bianca
Ay, but not frighted me; therefore I'll sleep again.

45 *Have at you*: be prepared.

46 *bird*: i.e. what you are hunting now.
shift my bush: go somewhere else.
47 *pursue . . . bow*: you will have to follow
me when you shoot.
48 *You . . . all*: The polite remark from a
hostess as she leads the ladies out.
49 *prevented me*: got there before me;
Petruchio concedes defeat.
Signor Tranio: For a moment Tranio
becomes a social equal with the other
gentlemen.
52 *slipped*: unleashed.

54 *swift*: quick-witted.
somewhat currish: rather more like a
mongrel (than a greyhound).
56 *deer*: Tranio puns on 'deer' and 'dear'; the
stag is said to be 'at bay' when it turns
and holds off the hounds.

58 *gird*: thrust.

60 *A*: he.
galled: touched.
61 *glance away*: bounce off.
62 *maimed*: wounded.

63 *good sadness*: quite seriously.
64 *veriest*: truest.

65 *for assurance*: to put it to the test.

Petruchio
Nay, that you shall not, since you have begun.
45 Have at you for a better jest—or two.
Bianca
Am I your bird? I mean to shift my bush,
And then pursue me as you draw your bow.
You are welcome all.
              [*Exeunt* Bianca, Katherina, *and* Widow
Petruchio
She hath prevented me. Here, Signor Tranio,
50 This bird you aimed at, though you hit her not;
Therefore a health to all that shot and missed.
Tranio
O sir, Lucentio slipped me like his greyhound,
Which runs himself, and catches for his master.
Petruchio
A good swift simile, but something currish.
Tranio
55 'Tis well, sir, that you hunted for yourself.
'Tis thought your deer does hold you at a bay.
Baptista
O, O, Petruchio! Tranio hits you now.
Lucentio
I thank thee for that gird, good Tranio.
Hortensio
Confess, confess, hath he not hit you here?
Petruchio
60 A has a little galled me, I confess;
And as the jest did glance away from me,
'Tis ten to one it maimed you two outright.
Baptista
Now, in good sadness, son Petruchio,
I think thou hast the veriest shrew of all.
Petruchio
65 Well, I say no. And therefore for assurance
Let's each one send unto his wife,
And he whose wife is most obedient,
To come at first when he doth send for her,
Shall win the wager which we will propose.
Hortensio
70 Content. What's the wager?
Lucentio   Twenty crowns.

72 *of*: on.

Petruchio
Twenty crowns?
I'll venture so much of my hawk or hound,
But twenty times so much upon my wife.
    Lucentio
A hundred then.
    Hortensio Content.
    Petruchio   A match, 'tis done.
    Hortensio
75 Who shall begin?
    Lucentio
That will I.
Go, Biondello, bid your mistress come to me.
    Biondello
I go.
                            [*Exit*

    Baptista

79 *be your half*: go halves with you (in the bet).

[*To* Lucentio] Son, I'll be your half Bianca comes.
    Lucentio
80 I'll have no halves; I'll bear it all myself.

        Enter Biondello

How now, what news?
    Biondello   Sir, my mistress sends you word
That she is busy, and she cannot come.
    Petruchio
How? 'She's busy, and she cannot come'?
Is that an answer?
    Gremio
                Ay, and a kind one too.
85 Pray God, sir, your wife send you not a worse.
    Petruchio
I hope better.
    Hortensio
Sirrah Biondello, go and entreat my wife
To come to me forthwith.
                   [*Exit* Biondello
    Petruchio   O ho, entreat her!

89 *must needs*: is sure to.

Nay, then she must needs come.

Hortensio   I am afraid, sir,
90 Do what you can [*Enter* Biondello] yours will not be
     entreated.
     Now where's my wife?
          Biondello
92 *you have . . . hand*: you're playing some   She says you have some goodly jest in hand.
funny trick.   She will not come; she bids you come to her.
          Petruchio
     Worse and worse; 'she will not come'! O vile,
95 Intolerable, not to be endured!
     Sirrah Grumio, go to your mistress,
     Say I command her come to me.
                                          [*Exit* Grumio
          Hortensio
     I know her answer.
          Petruchio   What?
          Hortensio   She will not.
          Petruchio
99 *there an end*: that's all there is to it.   The fouler fortune mine, and there an end.

                    Enter Katherina

          Baptista
100 *by my holidame*: by all that I hold sacred. 100 Now, by my holidame, here comes Katherina.
          Katherina
     What is your will, sir, that you send for me?
          Petruchio
     Where is your sister, and Hortensio's wife?
          Katherina
103 *conferring*: gossiping.   They sit conferring by the parlour fire.
          Petruchio
104 *deny*: refuse.   Go fetch them hither. If they deny to come,
105 *Swinge me . . . forth*: drive them out   105 Swinge me them soundly forth unto their husbands.
(Petruchio's words suggest the use of   Away, I say, and bring them hither straight.
physical force).   [*Exit* Katherina
          Lucentio
     Here is a wonder, if you talk of a wonder.
          Hortensio
     And so it is. I wonder what it bodes.
          Petruchio
     Marry, peace it bodes, and love, and quiet life,
110 *awful*: commanding great respect.   110 An awful rule, and right supremacy;
right: proper.   And, to be short, what not that's sweet and happy.
111 *what not that's*: everything else that is.

112 *fair befall thee*: good luck to you, congratulations.

114 *their losses*: i.e. the money that Lucentio and Hortensio have lost to Petruchio.

116 *as . . . been*: into a different person.

118 *show more sign*: give more evidence.

119 *new-built*: new-found; the repetition of 'obedience' in this line may be due to a printer's error (Shakespeare does not usually repeat himself without good reason).

120 *froward*: disobedient.

122 *becomes you not*: doesn't suit you.

123 *bauble*: piece of nonsense. *throw it under foot*: stamp on it.

125 *brought . . . pass*: forced to do such a silly thing.

130 *laying*: laying a bet.

137–80 Katherina's speech forms the climax of the play, articulating many Elizabethan commonplaces about marriage, yet appearing to spring directly from her own experience and feelings.

Baptista
Now fair befall thee, good Petruchio!
The wager thou hast won, and I will add
Unto their losses twenty thousand crowns,
115 Another dowry to another daughter,
For she is changed, as she had never been.

Petruchio
Nay, I will win my wager better yet,
And show more sign of her obedience,
Her new-built virtue and obedience.

Enter Katherina, Bianca, *and* Widow

120 See where she comes, and brings your froward wives
As prisoners to her womanly persuasion.
Katherine, that cap of yours becomes you not.
Off with that bauble, throw it under foot.

She obeys

Widow
Lord, let me never have a cause to sigh
125 Till I be brought to such a silly pass!

Bianca
Fie, what a foolish duty call you this?

Lucentio
I would your duty were as foolish too!
The wisdom of your duty, fair Bianca,
Hath cost me a hundred crowns since supper-time.

Bianca
130 The more fool you for laying on my duty.

Petruchio
Katherine, I charge thee tell these headstrong women
What duty they do owe their lords and husbands.

Widow
Come, come, you're mocking; we will have no telling.

Petruchio
Come on, I say, and first begin with her.

Widow
135 She shall not.

137 *unkind*: unfriendly; *and* unnatural.
138 *dart . . . eyes*: The image of wounding
darts shot from a mistress' eyes is a
commonplace of Elizabethan love poetry
— as are the allusions to meadows,
flowers, and fountains.
140 *blots*: stains.
meads: meadows.
141 *Confounds thy fame*: ruins your
reputation.
whirlwinds: In Sonnet xviii Shakespeare
described how 'Rough winds do shake the
darling buds of May' — i.e. blow the
buds off the trees.
142 *meet*: appropriate.
143 *moved*: bad-tempered.
144 *ill-seeming*: not worth looking at.
thick: not clear.
bereft: robbed.
145 *none . . . thirsty*: there is no-one, no
matter how dry or thirsty he may be.
148 *Thy head*: See Ephesians, 5:23: 'the
husband is the head of the wife, even as
Christ is the head of the Church.'
149 *maintenance*: support.
commits: risks.
150 *painful*: difficult, painstaking.
151 *watch*: be on watch through.
152 *secure*: free from worry.
153 *craves*: asks.
at thy hands: from you.
154 *fair*: kind.
156 *the subject*: See Ephesians, 5:24: 'as the
Church is subject unto Christ, so let the
wives be to their own husbands in
everything.'
160 *contending*: rebellious.
161 *graceless*: ungrateful.
162 *so simple*: so simple-minded as.
163 *offer*: declare.
167 *Unapt to*: unfitted for.
168 *soft conditions*: gentle natures.
170 *unable*: impotent.
171 *big*: arrogant.
one of yours: either of yours (that of
Bianca and of the Widow).
172 *heart*: i.e. the seat of courage.
haply: perhaps.
173 *bandy*: exchange, hit back and forth (as at
tennis).
175 *as weak*: i.e. as straws.
past compare: beyond comparison.
176 'Seeming to be most that (i.e. strong)
which in fact we are least.'

Petruchio
I say she shall: 'and first begin with her'.
    Katherina
Fie, fie, unknit that threatening unkind brow,
And dart not scornful glances from those eyes
To wound thy lord, thy king, thy governor.
140 It blots thy beauty, as frosts do bite the meads,
Confounds thy fame, as whirlwinds shake fair buds,
And in no sense is meet or amiable.
A woman moved is like a fountain troubled,
Muddy, ill-seeming, thick, bereft of beauty,
145 And while it is so, none so dry or thirsty
Will deign to sip or touch one drop of it.
Thy husband is thy lord, thy life, thy keeper,
Thy head, thy sovereign: one that cares for thee,
And for thy maintenance; commits his body
150 To painful labour both by sea and land,
To watch the night in storms, the day in cold,
Whilst thou liest warm at home, secure and safe,
And craves no other tribute at thy hands
But love, fair looks, and true obedience—
155 Too little payment for so great a debt.
Such duty as the subject owes the prince,
Even such, a woman oweth to her husband;
And when she is froward, peevish, sullen, sour,
And not obedient to his honest will,
160 What is she but a foul contending rebel
And graceless traitor to her loving lord?
I am ashamed that women are so simple
To offer war where they should kneel for peace;
Or seek for rule, supremacy, and sway
165 When they are bound to serve, love, and obey.
Why are our bodies soft, and weak, and smooth,
Unapt to toil and trouble in the world,
But that our soft conditions, and our hearts,
Should well agree with our external parts?
170 Come, come, you froward and unable worms,
My mind hath been as big as one of yours,
My heart as great, my reason haply more,
To bandy word for word and frown for frown;
But now I see our lances are but straws,
175 Our strength as weak, our weakness past compare,
That seeming to be most which we indeed least are.

177 *vail your stomachs*: stop being so proud of
   yourselves; 'vail' was used especially for
   the lowering of a ship's flag, and
   'stomach' was a common metaphor for
   conceit.
   it is no boot: there's nothing you can do
   about it.
178 *place . . . foot*: as a sign of submission.
181 *kiss me, Kate*: The words are used for
   the third time (compare *2,1,326*, and
   5,1,127); this time the kiss confirms
   their partnership.
182 *go thy ways*: well done.
   ha't: have it — the prize; Petruchio has
   won the wager.
183 *a good hearing*: good news.
   toward: obedient.
184 *a harsh hearing*: bad news.
   froward: wayward; the couplets which end
   the play are disappointingly banal.
186 *We three*: i.e. himself, Lucentio, and
   Hortensio.
   you two: i.e. Lucentio and Hortensio.
   sped: ruined.
187 *the white*: the centre of the target in
   archery; *also* Bianca, the Italian for
   'white'.
188 *being a winner*: whilst I am still winning.
190 *by your leave*: if you don't mind my
   saying so.

Then vail your stomachs, for it is no boot,
And place your hands below your husband's foot.
In token of which duty, if he please,
180 My hand is ready, may it do him ease.
       Petruchio
Why, there's a wench! Come on, and kiss me, Kate.
       Lucentio
Well, go thy ways, old lad, for thou shalt ha't.
       Vincentio
'Tis a good hearing when children are toward.
       Lucentio
But a harsh hearing when women are froward.
       Petruchio
185 Come, Kate, we'll to bed.
We three are married, but you two are sped.
[To *Lucentio*] 'Twas I won the wager, though you
   hit the white,
And being a winner, God give you good night!
                   [*Exeunt* Petruchio *and* Katherina
       Hortensio
Now go thy ways, thou hast tamed a curst shrew.
       Lucentio
190 'Tis a wonder, by your leave, she will be tamed so.
                                          [*Exeunt*

Appendix A

Christopher Sly

After *Act 1*, Scene I of *The Taming of The Shrew*, Shakespeare seems to have forgotten about Christopher Sly and the trickster Lord. But a dramatist completed the deception of the tinker in *The Taming of A Shrew*, a play which seems to be an imitation of Shakespeare's. Here the Lord is addressed as 'Sim' — Simon — although it is possible that this was the name of the actor who played the part. These are the major episodes which complete the 'framework'.

1. *A Shrew*, scene v — after the marriage with Kate has been arranged.
        Then Sly *speaks*
    Sly
    Sim, when will the fool come again?
        Lord
    He'll come again, my lord, anon.
        Sly
    Gi's some more drink here. Zounds, where's the tapster?
    Here, Sim, eat some of these things.
        Lord
    So I do, my lord.
        Sly
    Here, Sim: I drink to thee!
        Lord
    My lord, here comes the players again.
        Sly
    O brave! Here's two fine gentlewomen.

2. *A Shrew*, scene xiv — following the marriage of Kate's two sisters.
        Sly
    Sim, must they be married now?
        Lord
    Ay, my lord.
        Sly
    Look, Sim, the fool is come again now.

3.   *A Shrew*, scene xvi — the imposters are condemned to prison, and they run away — compare, 5, 1, 98 *s.d.*

> *Then* Sly *speaks*

Sly

I say we'll have no sending to prison.

Lord

My lord, this is but the play; they're but in jest.

Sly

I tell thee Sim, we'll have no sending to prison, that's flat. Why, Sim, am I not Don Christo Vary? Therefore I say they shall not go to prison.

Lord

No more they shall, my lord; they be run away.

Sly

Are they run away, Sim? That's well. Then gi's some more to drink, and let them play again.

> Sly *drinks, and then falls asleep*

4.   *A Shrew*, scene xvi — between *Act 5* scenes 1 and 2 of *The Shrew*.

> Sly *sleeps*

Lord

Who's within there? Come hither sirs; my lord's
Asleep again; go, take him easily up,
And put him in his own apparel again,
And lay him in the place where we did find him
Just underneath the alehouse side below.
But see you wake him not in any case.

Boy

It shall be done, my lord. Come, help to bear him hence.

5.   *A Shrew*, scene xix — an Epilogue to the main action.
Then enter two bearing Sly *in his own apparel again, and leaves him where they found him; and then goes out.*

> *Then enter the* Tapster

Tapster

Now that the darksome night is overpast,
And dawning day appears in crystal sky,
Now must I haste abroad. But soft, who's this?
What, Sly! O wondrous, hath he lain here all night?
I'll wake him: I think he's starved by this,
But that his belly was so stuffed with ale.
What, how, Sly! Awake, for shame!

Sly

Sim, gi's some more wine — what's all the players gone? Am I not a lord?

Tapster

A lord with a murrain! Come, art thou drunken still?

Sly

Who's this? Tapster! O Lord, sirrah, I have had the bravest dream tonight that ever thou heardest in all thy life.

Tapster

Ay, marry, but you had best get you home, for your wife will curse you for dreaming here tonight.

Sly

Will she? I know now how to tame a shrew: I dreamed upon it all this night till now, and thou hast waked me out of the best dream that ever I had in my life. But I'll to my wife presently, and tame her too, if she anger me.

Tapster

Nay, tarry Sly, for I'll go home with thee,
And hear the rest that thou hast dreamed tonight.

Exeunt omnes

Appendix B

Manning a Hawk

In *Act 4*, Scene 1 Petruchio describes Katherina as a 'haggard' — a wild hawk. Confiding in the audience, he describes the strategies he will employ 'to man my haggard, To make her come and know her keeper's call' (181–2). His methods would be familiar to his Elizabethan audience — and they are still in use today.

Gervase Markham, in *Country Pursuits* (1615), describes the standard technique for training a wild hawk in order to make her 'meek and loving to the man':

> All hawks generally are manned after one manner, that is to say, by watching and keeping them from sleep, by a continual carrying of them upon your fist, and by a most familiar stroking and playing with them, with the wing of a dead fowl or such like, and by often gazing and looking of them in the face, with a loving and gentle countenance, and so making them acquainted with the man.

In *A Kestrel for a Knave*, by Barry Hines (Michael Joseph, 1968), Billy Casper describes the same process to his schoolmates. The scene is a schoolroom in an industrial town in the north of England, sometime in the middle of the twentieth century.

Mr Farthing rested his elbows on his desk and tapped his teeth with his thumb nails, waiting for Billy to collect himself.

    'Now then, Billy, tell us about this hawk. Where did you get it from?'

    'Found it.'

    'Where?'

    'In t'wood.'

    'What had happened to it? Was it injured or something?'

    'It was a young 'un. It must have tumbled from a nest.'

    'And how long have you had it?'

    'Since last year.'

    'All that time? Where do you keep it?'

    'In a shed.'

'And what do you feed it on?'

'Beef. Mice. Birds.'

'Isn't it cruel though, keeping it in a shed all the time? Wouldn't it be happier flying free?'

Billy looked at Mr Farthing for the first time since he had told him to sit down.

'I don't keep it in t'shed all t'time. I fly it every day.'

'And doesn't it fly away? I thought hawks were wild birds.'

''Course it don't fly away. I've trained it.'

Billy looked round, as though daring anyone to challenge this authority.

'Trained it? I thought you'd to be an expert to train hawks.'

'Well I did it.'

'Was it difficult?'

''Course it was. You've to be right . . . right patient wi' 'em and take your time.'

'Well tell me how you did it then. I've never met a falconer before, I suppose I must be in select company.'

Billy hutched his chair up and leaned forward over his desk.

'Well what you do is, you train 'em through their stomachs. You can only do owt wi' 'em when they're hungry, so you do all your training at feeding times.

'I started training Kes after I'd had her about a fortnight, when she was hard penned, that means her tail feathers and wing feathers had gone hard at their bases. You have to use a torch at night and keep inspecting 'em. It's easy if you're quiet, you just go up to her as she's roosting, and spread her tail and wings. If t'feathers are blue near t'bottom o' t'shaft, that means there's blood in 'em and they're still soft, so they're not ready yet. When they're white and hard then they're ready, an' you can start training her then.

'Kes wa' as fat as a pig though at first. All young hawks are when you first start to train 'em, and you can't do much wi' 'em 'til you've got their weight down. You've to be ever so careful though, you don't just starve 'em, you weigh 'em before every meal and gradually cut their food down, 'til you go in one time an' she's keen, an' that's when you start getting somewhere. I could tell wi' Kes, she jumped straight on my glove as I held it towards her. So while she wa' feeding I got hold of her jesses an' . . .'

'Her what?'

'Jesses.'

'Jesses. How do you spell that?'

Mr Farthing stood up and stepped back to the board.

'Er, J-E-S-S-E-S.'

As Billy enunciated each letter, Mr Farthing linked them together on the blackboard.

'Jesses. And what are jesses, Billy?'

'They're little leather straps that you fasten round its legs as soon as you get it. She wears these all t'time, and you get hold of 'em when she sits on your glove. You push your swivel through . . .'

'Whoa! Whoa!'

Mr Farthing held up his hands as though Billy was galloping towards him.

'You'd better come out here and give us a demonstration. We're not all experts you know.'

Billy stood up and walked out, taking up position at the side of Mr Farthing's desk. Mr Farthing reared his chair on to its back legs, swivelled it sideways on one leg, then lowered it on to all fours facing Billy.

'Right, off you go.'

'Well, when she stands on your fist, you pull her jesses down between your fingers.'

Billy held his left fist out and drew the jesses down between his first and second fingers.

'Then you get your swivel, like a swivel on a dog lead, press both jesses together, and thread 'em through t'top ring of it. T'jesses have little slits in 'em near t'bottom, like buttonholes in braces, and when you've got t'jesses through t'top ring o' t'swivel, you open these slits with your finger, and push t'bottom ring through, just like fastening a button.'

With the swivel now attached to the jesses, Billy turned to Mr Farthing.

'Do you see?'

'Yes, I see. Carry on.'

'Well when you've done that, you thread your leash, that's a leather thong, through t'bottom ring o' t'swivel . . .'

Billy carefully threaded the leash, grabbed the loose end as it penetrated the ring, and pulled it through.

'. . . until it binds on t'knot at t'other end. Have you got that?'

'Yes, I think so. Just let me get it right. The jesses round the hawk's legs are attached to a swivel, which is then attached to a lead . . .'

'A leash!'

'Leash, sorry. Then what?'

'You wrap your leash round your fingers and tie it on to your little finger.'

'So that the hawk is now attached to your hand?'

'That's right. Well, when you've reached this stage and it's stepping on to your glove regular, and feeding all right and not bating too much . . .'

'Bating? What's that?'

'Trying to fly off; in a panic like.'

'How do you spell it?'

'B-A-T-I-N-G.'

'Carry on.'

'Well, when you've reached this stage inside, you can try feeding her outside and getting her used to other things. You call this manning. That means taming, and you've got to have her well manned before you can start training her right.'

While Billy was talking, Mr Farthing reached out and slowly printed on the board B A T I N G; watching Billy all the time as though he was a hawk, and that any sudden movement, or rasp of chalk would make him bate from the side of the desk.

'You take her out at night first and don't go near anybody. I used to walk her round t'fields at t'back of our house at first, then as she got less nervous I started to bring her out in t'day and then take her near other folks, and dogs and cats and cars and things. You've to be ever so careful when you're outside though, 'cos hawks are right nervous and they've got fantastic eyesight, and things are ten times worse for them than they are for us. So you've to be right patient, an' all t'time you're walking her you've to talk to her, all soft like, like you do to a baby.'

He paused for breath. Mr Farthing nodded him on before he had time to become self-conscious.

'Well, when you've manned her, you can start training her right then. You can tell when she's ready, 'cos she looks forward to you comin' an' there's no trouble gettin' her on to your glove. Not like at first when she's bating all t'time.

'You start inside first, makin' her jump on to your glove for her meat. Only a little jump at first, then a bit further and so on; and every time she comes you've to give her a scrap o' meat. A reward like. When she'll come about a leash length straight away, you can try her outside, off a fence post or summat like that. You put her down, hold on to t'end of your leash wi' your right hand, and hold your glove out for her to fly to. This way you can get a double leash length. After she's done this, you can take her leash off an' attach a creance in its place.'

'Creance?'

Mr Farthing leaned over to the blackboard.

'C-R-E-A-N-C-E — it's a long line, I used a long nylon fishing line wi' a clasp off a dog lead, tied to one end. Well, you clip this to your swivel, pull your leash out, and put your hawk down on a fence post. Then you walk away into t'field unwindin' your creance, an' t'hawk sits there waitin' for you to stop an' hold your glove up. It's so it can't fly away, you see.'

'Yes I see. It all sounds very skilful and complicated, Billy.'

'It don't sound half as bad as it is though. I've just told you in a couple o' minutes how to carry on, but it takes weeks to go through all them stages. They're as stubborn as mules, hawks, they're right tempr . . . tempr . . .'

'Temperamental.'

'Temperamental. Sometimes she'd be all right, then next time I'd go in, she'd go mad, screamin' an' batin' as though she'd never seen me before. You'd think you'd learnt her summat, an' put her away feelin' champion, then t'next time you went you were back where you started. You just couldn't reckon it up at all.'

He looked down at Mr Farthing, eyes animated, cheeks flushed under a wash of smeared tears and dirt.

'You make it sound very exciting though.'

'It is, Sir. But most exciting thing wa' when I flew her free first time. You ought to have been there then. I wa' frightened to death.'

Mr Farthing turned to the class, rotating his trunk without moving his chair.

'Do you want to hear about it?'

Chorus: 'Yes, Sir.'

Mr Farthing smiled and turned back to Billy.

'Carry on, Casper.'

'Well I'd been flyin' it on t'creance for about a week, an' it wa' comin' back to me owt up to thirty, forty yards, an' it says in t'books that when it's comin' this far, straight away, it's ready to fly loose. I daren't though. I kep' sayin' to missen, I'll just use t'creance today to make sure, then I'll fly it free tomorrow. But when tomorrow came I did t'smack same thing. I did this for about four days an' I got right mad wi' missen 'cos I knew I'd have to do it sometime. So on t'last day I didn't feed her up, just to make sure that she'd be sharp set next morning. I hardly went to sleep that night, I wa' thinking about it that much.

'It wa' on Friday night, an' when I got up next morning I thought right, if she flies off, she flies off, an' it can't be helped. So I went down to t'shed. She wa' dead keen an' all, walking about on her shelf behind t'bars, an' screamin' out when she saw me comin'. So I took her out in t'field and tried her on t'creance first time, an' she came like a rocket. So I thought, right, this time.

'I unclipped t'creance, took t'swivel off an' let her hop on to t'fence post. There was nowt stoppin' her now, she wa' just standin' there wi' her jesses on. She could have took off an' there wa' nowt I could have done about it. I wa' terrified. I thought she's forced to go, she's forced to, she'll just fly an' that'll be it. But she didn't. She just sat there looking round while I backed off into t'field. I went right into t'middle, then held my glove up an' shouted her.'

Billy held his left fist up and stared out of the window.

'Come on, Kes! Come on then! Nowt happened at first, then, just when I wa' going to walk back to her, she came. You ought to have seen her. Straight as a die, about a yard off t'floor. An' t'speed . . . She came like lightnin', head dead still, an' her wings never made a sound, then wham! Straight up on to t'glove, claws out grabbin' for t'meat,' simultaneously demonstrating the last yard of her flight with his right hand, gliding it towards, then slapping it down on his raised fist.

'I wa' that pleased I didn't know what to do wi' missen, so I thought just to prove it, I'll try her again, an' she came t'second time just as good. Well that was it. I'd done it. I'd trained her.'

(This extract is published by kind permission of Michael Joseph Ltd, © 1968 by Barry Hines.)

Classwork and Examinations

The works of Shakespeare are studied all over the world, and this classroom edition is being used in many different countries. Teaching methods vary from school to school and there are many different ways of examining a student's work. Some teachers and examiners expect detailed knowledge of Shakespeare's text; others ask for imaginative involvement with his characters and their situations; and there are some teachers who want their students to share in the theatrical experience of directing and performing a play. Most people use a variety of methods. This section of the book offers a few suggestions for approaches to *The Taming of the Shrew* which could be used in schools and colleges to help with students' understanding and *enjoyment* of the play.

 A Discussion
 B Character Study
 C Activities
 D Context Questions
 E Comprehension Questions
 F Essays
 G Projects

A   Discussion

Talking about the play — about the issues it raises and the characters who are involved — is one of the most rewarding and pleasurable aspects of the study of Shakespeare. It makes sense to discuss each scene as it is read, sharing impressions — and perhaps correcting misapprehensions. It can be useful to compare aspects of this play with other fictions — plays, novels, films — or with modern life.

Suggestions

A1   Christopher Sly has 'never heard a play' (*Induction*, Scene 1, line 95). How would you describe plays — both comedies and tragedies — to somone who knows nothing about drama? Are plays anything more than entertainment? Is there any difference between seeing a play at the theatre and watching a film at the cinema or on television?

A2 Baptista arranges the marriages of both his daughters. Can you think of any other 'arranged marriages' in fiction? Do such marriages happen in the twentieth century? Do you think parents should be able to influence their children in this way?

A3 Tranio asks 'is it possible That love should of a sudden take such hold?' (*1*, 1, 143–4). Do you believe in love at first sight?

A4 Baptista arranges for his daughters to have tuition in literature and music. Do you think it is necessary to have some knowledge of arts subjects?

A5 Some of Shakespeare's characters (for instance Gremio, the 'pantaloon') are well-known stock figures from the conventions of the *commedia dell'arte*. What character stereotypes do we recognize today — in plays, films, and television?

A6 If you were to stage this play, would you put the characters in modern dress? What would be the advantages and the drawbacks?

B   Character Study

Shakespeare is famous for his creation of characters who seem like real people. We can judge their actions and we can try to understand their thoughts and feelings — just as we criticize and try to understand the people we know. As the play progresses, we learn to like or dislike, love or hate, them — just as though they lived in *our* world.

Characters can be studied *from the outside*, by observing what they do, and listening sensitively to what they say. This is the scholar's method: the scholar — or any reader — has access to the whole play, and can see the function of every character within the whole scheme of that play.

Another approach works *from the inside*, taking a single character and looking at the action and the other characters from his/her point of view. This is an actor's technique, creating a character — who can have only a partial view of what is going on — for performance; and it asks for a student's inventive imagination. The two methods — both useful in different ways — are really complementary to each other.

Suggestions

a) from 'outside' the character

B1 Write detailed character studies of
a) Bianca
b) Katherina
c) Petruchio

B2 At the beginning of the play, Petruchio is a fortune-hunter who has 'come to wive it wealthily in Padua' (*1*, 2, 74). Show how the character develops from this point.

B3 'They deserve each other.' Could this be said of *either* Katherina and Petruchio, *or* Bianca and Lucentio?

B4 Ben Jonson (a contemporary dramatist) said that Shakespeare 'was not of an age, but for all time'. What 'timeless' qualities do you particularly notice in the characters of *The Taming of the Shrew*?

B5 What functions are served by the comic servants (Tranio, Grumio, and Biondello)?

b) from 'inside' a character

B6 As Baptista, write letters to an old friend in another town describing:
a) your two daughters and your hopes (and fears) about their futures.
b) the wedding of Katherina.
c) the amazing transformation of Katherina after her marriage.

B7 In the character of Bianca, writing to a girl-friend, describe
a) your sister.
b) your new tutors.
c) Katherina's wedding.

B8 In Katherina's personal diary, confide your thoughts about
a) your father.
b) your sister and her suitors.
c) Petruchio, both before and after your wedding.

B9 As one of Petruchio's other servants (i.e. *not* Grumio), describe your master's treatment of his new bride.

B10 Write a letter from the Widow (Hortensio's bride) to one of her old friends, describing the events and personalities at the wedding feast.

C Activities

These can involve two or more students, preferably working *away from* the desk or study-table and using gesture and position ('body-language') as well as speech. They can help students to develop a sense of drama and the dramatic aspects of Shakespeare's play — which was written to be *performed*, not studied in a classroom.

Suggestions

C1 Act the play, or at least some parts of it (e.g. the first encounter — *Act 2*, Scene 1 — of Katherina and Petruchio).

C2 Devise some new scenes with Christopher Sly to complete the 'framework' of the play (see Appendix A, p. 101).

C3 Baptista is an important man in Padua, and the wedding of his elder daughter would be widely reported. Give it full 'media coverage' (newspaper, radio, and television), interviewing all who were present — including those who saw nothing but want to appear on television. Research a background for 'The Mysterious Stranger from Verona'.

C4   When it comes, will it come without warning
            Just as I'm picking my nose?
    Will it knock on my door in the morning,
            Or tread in the bus on my toes?
    Will it come like a change in the weather?
            Will its greeting be courteous or rough?
    Will it alter my life altogether?
            O tell me the truth about love.
                                    (W.H. Auden, Song XII)

Organize a classroom debate to answer Auden's question. How would the different male characters — Lucentio, Gremio, Hortensio, and Petruchio — answer? Would Katherina or Bianca be able to tell 'the truth about love'? Is Baptista interested in love? What is the Widow's point of view?

C5 Let one member of the group read aloud Katherina's exhortation to wives ('Fie, fie, unknit that threat'ning, unkind brow', 5, 2, 137–80) whilst the rest *listen*; then let the others — either representing characters in the play or in their own persons — describe their reactions — how they thought and felt at the time the speech was being read, and what they think afterwards.

D   Context Questions

In written examinations, these questions present you with short passages from the play, and ask you to explain them. They are intended to test your knowledge of the play and your understanding of its words. Usually you have to make a choice of passages: there may be five on the paper, and you are asked to choose three. Be very sure that you know exactly how many passages you must choose. Study the ones offered to you, and select those you feel most certain of. Make your answers accurate and concise — don't waste time writing more than the examiner is asking for.

D1   Am I a lord, and have I such a lady?
Or do I dream? Or have I dreamed till now?
I do not sleep: I see, I hear, I speak,
I smell sweet savours and I feel soft things.
Upon my life, I am a lord indeed,

   (i) Who is speaking?
   (ii) Who is the 'lady' he refers to?
   (iii) Where is he speaking from, and how did he get there?

D2   Why, sir, you know this is your wedding-day.
First were we sad, fearing you would not come,
Now sadder, that you come so unprovided.
Fie, doff this habit, shame to your estate,
An eyesore to our solemn festival!

   (i) Who is the speaker, and to whom is he speaking?
   (ii) How is this person 'unprovided'?
   (iii) What happens next?

D3   Mistake no more, I am not Litio,
Nor a musician as I seem to be,
But one that scorn to live in this disguise
For such a one as leaves a gentleman
And makes a god of such a cullion.

   (i) What is the speaker's real name?
   (ii) Who is referred to as 'such a one', and who is described
        as a 'cullion'?
   (iii) Whom does the speaker marry?

D4   But after many ceremonies done
He calls for wine. 'A health!' quoth he, as if
He had been aboard, carousing to his mates
After a storm; quaffed off the muscadel,
And threw the sops all in the sexton's face,

(i) Who is the speaker, and to whom is he speaking?
(ii) What 'ceremonies' have been performed?
(iii) Who is the person referred to as 'He'?

D5   I am my father's heir and only son;
If I may have your daughter to my wife,
I'll leave her houses three or four as good
Within rich Pisa walls as any one
Old Signor – – has in – –.

(i) What are the real and assumed names of the speaker?
(ii) To whom is he speaking, and which 'daughter' does he refer to?
(iii) Who is the 'Old Signor', and in which town are his 'houses'?

E   Comprehension Questions

These also present passages from the play and ask questions about them, and again you often have a choice of passages. But the extracts are much longer than those presented as context questions. A detailed knowledge of the language of the play is asked for here, and you must be able to express unusual or archaic phrases in your own words; you may also be asked to comment critically on the effectiveness of Shakespeare's language.

E1   *Petruchio*
Well, come my Kate, we will unto your father's
Even in these honest mean habiliments.
Our purses shall be proud, our garments poor,
For 'tis the mind that makes the body rich;
And as the sun breaks through the darkest clouds,
So honour peereth in the meanest habit.   5
What, is the jay more precious than the lark
Because his painted skin contents the eye?

O no, good Kate; neither art thou the worse
For this poor furniture and mean array.   10
If thou account'st it shame, lay it on me,
And therefore frolic: we will hence forthwith
To feast and sport us at thy father's house.

   (i) Why is Kate 'in mean array'? Will the characters go
      immediately to Padua?
  (ii) What is meant by 'will unto your father's' (line 1); 'mean
      habiliments' (line 2); 'lay it on me' (line 11).
 (iii) Express in your own words the meaning of line 3 'Our
      purses . . . poor' and line 6 'honour . . . habit'.
 (iv) Comment on the style of this speech. What impression is
      Petruchio trying to make?

E2 *Tranio*
Softly, my masters! If you be gentlemen,
Do me this right; hear me with patience.
Baptista is a noble gentleman,
To whom my father is not all unknown,
And were his daughter fairer than she is,   5
She may more suitors have, and me for one.
Fair Leda's daughter had a thousand wooers,
Then well one more may fair Bianca have;
And so she shall: Lucentio shall make one,
Though Paris came, in hope to speed alone.   10

   (i) To whom is Tranio speaking? How does he try to
      impress them?
  (ii) Who were 'Leda's daughter' and 'Paris'?
 (iii) What is meant by 'Softly' (line 1); 'Do me this right' (line
      2); 'speed' (line 10).

E3 *Petruchio*
Thus have I politicly begun my reign,
And 'tis my hope to end successfully.
My falcon now is sharp and passing empty,
And till she stoop she must not be full-gorged,
For then she never looks upon her lure.   5
Another way I have to man my haggard,
To make her come and know her keeper's call:
That is, to watch her, as we watch these kites
That bate and beat and will not be obedient.

She ate no meat today, nor none shall eat.   10
Last night she slept not, nor tonight she shall not.
As with the meat, some undeserved fault
I'll find about the making of the bed,
And here I'll fling the pillow, there the bolster,
This way the coverlet, another way the sheets.   15
Ay, and amid this hurly I intend
That all is done in reverent care of her.
And, in conclusion, she shall watch all night,
And if she chance to nod I'll rail and brawl,
And with the clamour keep her still awake.   20
This is the way to kill a wife with kindness,
And thus I'll curb her mad and headstrong humour.

(i) To whom is this speech addressed? Why is Petruchio speaking in this way?

(ii) What is the meaning of 'passing empty' (line 3); 'to watch' (line 8); 'kites' (line 8); 'hurly' (line 16); 'rail' (line 19).

(iii) Express in your own words the sense of lines 1–2 ('Thus have I . . . successfully'), and lines 4–5 ('till . . . lure').

(iv) Petruchio compares Katherina with a hawk. In your opinion, is this comparison effective?

F Essays

These will usually give you a specific topic to discuss, or perhaps a question that must be answered, in writing, *with a reasoned argument*. They *never* want you to tell the story of the play — so don't! Your examiner — or teacher — has read the play and does not need to be reminded of it. Relevant quotations will always help you to make your points more strongly.

Suggested Topics

F1 ''Tis a wonder, by your leave, she will be tamed so' (5, 2, 190). Do you share Lucentio's scepticism about the success of Petruchio's 'taming' of Katherina?

F2 Do you think — on the evidence of this play — that Shakespeare was anti-feminist?

F3 Examine Shakespeare's use of prose and verse in *The Taming of the Shrew*.

F4 Do you agree with Anne Barton that 'at the end of the play, Katherina is a woman who has discovered, and come to terms with, her own genuine nature'?

F5 Discuss the theme of appearance and reality in *The Taming of the Shrew*.

G   Projects

In some schools, students are asked to do more 'free-ranging' work, which takes them outside the text — but which should always be relevant to the play. Such Projects may demand skills other than reading and writing; design and artwork, for instance, may be involved. Sometimes a 'portfolio' of work is assembled over a considerable period of time; and this can be presented to the examiner as part of the student's work for assessment.

The availability of resources will, obviously, do much to determine the nature of the Projects; but this is something that only the local teachers will understand. However, there is always help to be found in libraries, museums, and art galleries.

G1 Arranged marriages.

G2 Past productions of *The Taming of the Shrew*.

G3 Costumes for *The Taming of the Shrew*.

G4 'The Battle of the Sexes'.

G5 The *Commedia dell'arte*.

G6 Actors on Tour.

Background

England c. 1592

When Shakespeare was writing *The Taming of the Shrew*, most people believed that the sun went round the earth. They were taught that this was a divinely ordered scheme of things, and that — in England — God had instituted a Church and ordained a Monarchy for the right government of the land and the populace.

'The past is a foreign country; they do things differently there.'

L.P. Hartley

Government

For most of Shakespeare's life, the reigning monarch of England was Queen Elizabeth I. With her counsellors and ministers, she governed the country (population about five million) from London, although fewer than half a million people inhabited the capital city. In the rest of the country, law and order were maintained by the land-owners and enforced by their deputies. The average man had no vote — and his wife had no rights at all.

Religion

At this time, England was a Christian country. All children were baptized, soon after they were born, into the Church of England; they were taught the essentials of the Christian faith, and instructed in their duty to God and to humankind. Marriages were performed, and funerals conducted, only by the licensed clergy and in accordance with the Church's rites and ceremonies. Attendance at divine service was compulsory; absences (without good — medical — reason) could be punished by fines. By such means, the authorities were able to keep some check on the populace — recording births, marriages, and deaths; being alert to any religious nonconformity, which could be politically dangerous; and ensuring a minimum of orthodox instruction through the official 'Homilies' which were regularly preached from the pulpits of all parish churches throughout the realm. Following Henry VIII's break away from the Church of Rome, all people in England were able to hear the church services *in their own language*. The Book of Common Prayer was used in every church, and an English translation of the Bible was read aloud in public. The Christian religion had never been so well taught before!

Education

School education reinforced the Church's teaching. From the age of four, boys might attend the 'petty school' (French *'petite école'*) to learn the rudiments of reading and writing along with a few prayers; some schools also included work with numbers. At the age of seven, the boy was ready for the grammar school (if his father was willing and able to pay the fees).

Here, a thorough grounding in Latin grammar was followed by translation work and the study of Roman authors, paying attention as much to style as to matter. The arts of fine writing were thus inculcated from early youth. A very few students proceeded to university; these were either clever scholarship boys, or else the sons of noblemen. Girls stayed at home, and acquired domestic and social skills — cooking, sewing, perhaps even music. The lucky ones might learn to read and write.

Language

At the start of the sixteenth century the English had a very poor opinion of their own language: there was little serious writing in English, and hardly any literature. Latin was the language of international scholarship, and Englishmen admired the eloquence of the Romans. They made many translations, and in this way they extended the resources of their own language, increasing its vocabulary and stretching its grammatical structures. French, Italian, and Spanish works were also translated, and — for the first time — there were English versions of the Bible. By the end of the century, English was a language to be proud of: it was rich in synonyms, capable of infinite variety and subtlety, and ready for all kinds of word-play — especially the *puns*, for which Shakespeare's English is renowned.

Drama

The great art-form of the Elizabethan age was its drama. The Elizabethans inherited a tradition of play-acting from the Middle Ages, and they reinforced this by reading and translating the Roman playwrights. At the beginning of the sixteenth century, plays were performed by groups of actors, all-male companies (boys acted the female roles) who travelled from town to town, setting up their stages in open places (such as inn-yards) or, with the permission of the owner, in the hall of some noble house. The touring companies continued, in the provinces, into the seventeenth century; but in London, in 1576, a new building was erected for the performance of plays. This was the Theatre, the first purpose-built playhouse in England. Other playhouses followed (including Shakespeare's own theatre, the Globe); and the English drama reached new heights of eloquence.

There were those who disapproved, of course. The theatres, which brought large crowds together, could encourage the spread of disease — and dangerous ideas. During the summer, when the plague was at its worst, the playhouses were closed. A constant censorship was imposed, more or less severe at different times. The Puritan faction tried to close down the theatres, but — partly because there was royal favour for the drama, and partly because the buildings were outside the city limits — they did not succeed until 1642.

Theatre

From contemporary comments and sketches — most particularly a drawing by a Dutch visitor, Johannes de Witt — it is possible to form some idea of the typical Elizabethan playhouse for which most of Shakespeare's plays were written. Hexagonal in shape, it had three roofed galleries encircling an open courtyard. The plain, high stage projected into the yard, where it was surrounded by the audience of standing 'groundlings'. At the back were two doors for the actors' entrances and exits; and above these doors was a balcony — useful for a musicians' gallery or for the acting of scenes 'above'. Over the stage was a thatched roof, supported on two pillars, forming a canopy — which seems to have been painted with the sun, moon and stars for the 'heavens'.

Underneath was space (concealed by curtaining) which could be used by characters ascending and descending through a trap-door in the stage. Costumes and properties were kept backstage, in the 'tiring house'. The actors dressed lavishly, often wearing the secondhand clothes bestowed by rich patrons. Stage properties were important for defining a location, but the dramatist's own words were needed to explain the time of day, since all performances took place in the early afternoon.

Selected Further Reading

Berry, Ralph, *Shakespeare's Comedies*, (Princeton University Press, 1972).

Dusinberre, Juliet, *Shakespeare and the Nature of Women*, (London, 1975).

Leggatt, Alexander, *Shakespeare's Comedy of Love*, (London, 1974).

Muir, Kenneth, *The Sources of Shakespeare's Plays*, (London, 1977).

Nevo, Ruth, *Comic Transformations in Shakespeare*, (Methuen, 1980).

Salinger, Leo, *Shakespeare and the Traditions of Comedy*, (Cambridge, 1974).

Stone, Lawrence, *The Family, Sex and Marriage in England, 1500–1800*, (1977).

Background Reading

Blake, N.F., *Shakespeare's Language: an Introduction*, (Methuen, 1983).

Muir, K., and Schoenbaum, S., *A New Companion to Shakespeare Studies*, (Cambridge, 1971).

Schoenbaum, S., *William Shakespeare: A Documentary Life*, (Oxford, 1975).

Thomson, Peter, *Shakespeare's Theatre*, (Routledge and Kegan Paul, 1983).

William Shakespeare, 1564–1616

Elizabeth I was Queen of England when Shakespeare was born in 1564. He was the son of a tradesman who made and sold gloves in the small town of Stratford-upon-Avon, and he was educated at the grammar school in that town. Shakespeare did not go to university when he left school, but worked, perhaps, in his father's business. When he was eighteen he married Anne Hathaway, who became the mother of his daughter, Susanna, in 1583, and of twins in 1585.

There is nothing exciting, or even unusual, in this story; and from 1585 until 1592 there are no documents that can tell us anything at all about Shakespeare. But we have learned that in 1592 he was known in London, and that he had become both an actor and a playwright.

We do not know when Shakespeare wrote his first play, and indeed we are not sure of the order in which he wrote his works. If you look on page 125 at the list of his writings and their approximate dates, you will see how he started by writing plays on subjects taken from the history of England. No doubt this was partly because he was always an intensely patriotic man—but he was also a very shrewd business-man. He could see that the theatre audiences enjoyed being shown their own history, and it was certain that he would make a profit from this kind of drama.

The plays in the next group are mainly comedies, with romantic love stories of young people who fall in love with one another, and at the end of the play marry and live happily ever after.

At the end of the sixteenth century the happiness disappears, and Shakespeare's plays become melancholy, bitter, and tragic. This change may have been caused by some sadness in the writer's life (one of his twins died in 1596). Shakespeare, however, was not the only writer whose works at this time were very serious. The whole of England was facing a crisis. Queen Elizabeth I was growing old. She was greatly loved, and the people were sad to think she must soon die; they were also afraid, for the Queen had never married, and so there was no child to succeed her.

When James I came to the throne in 1603, Shakespeare continued to write serious drama—the great tragedies and the plays based on Roman history (such as *Julius Caesar*) for which he is most famous. Finally, before he retired from the theatre, he wrote another set of comedies. These all have the same theme: they tell of happiness which is lost, and then found again.

Shakespeare returned from London to Stratford, his home town. He was rich and successful, and he owned one of the biggest houses in the town. He died in 1616.

Shakespeare also wrote two long poems, and a collection of sonnets. The sonnets describe two love-affairs, but we do not know who the lovers were. Although there are many public documents concerned with his career as a writer and a business-man, Shakespeare has hidden his personal life from us. A nineteenth-century poet, Matthew Arnold, addressed Shakespeare in a poem, and wrote 'We ask and ask—Thou smilest, and art still'.

There is not even a trustworthy portrait of the world's greatest dramatist.